UPDATING THE CONSTITUTION

Applying 250 Years of Experience with One of the World's Most Important Documents

---

by Carl D. Veley

DORRANCE
PUBLISHING CO
EST. 1920
PITTSBURGH, PENNSYLVANIA 15238

Dorrance Publishing Co
585 Alpha Drive
Pittsburgh, PA 15238
Visit our website at *www.dorrancebookstore.com*

ISBN: 978-1-6495-7126-7
eISBN: 978-1-6495-7633-0

Table of Contents

CARL D. VELEY

UPDATING THE CONSTITUTION

Synopsis

Voting kills Democracy. We call a country a Democracy if it selects its leaders through elections, where all eligible citizens cast a ballot. Superficially that appears to be a Majority-Rule system with ordinary people, through their representatives, making laws and deciding policies. A closer look reveals that technology and political chicanery have so contaminated voting processes that elected Representatives do not in fact represent their constituents, and Majority-Rule has devolved into a type of government the Constitution was intended to prevent.

There are two important factors that prevent contemporary elections from attaining their objectives. First is the inculcating power of advertising and its contribution to polarizing opinions and obstructing rational debate. Second, we want laws and policies decided by ordinary people, but ordinary people seldom, if ever, become our representatives. The cost of campaigning is so high that people who run for office are themselves very wealthy or have backing from wealthy zealots who expect something in return for their investment. Also, those who seek a role in legislation tend to be more fanatical than most people. They can hardly be considered typical of ordinary people.

The United States Constitution was brilliant when it was written, but that was in the 18th century and there have been incredible changes in technology, sociology, and language since then. It is time to rethink the document and learn from two centuries of experience.

We are proposing an election system wherein a statistically significant number of voters (a proxy panel) are selected at random by computer searching a detailed database. When done properly, this group would be demographically representative of the entire populace but would be small enough that it could be sequestered and temporarily shielded from harangues of partisan politics. The group could be informed and compelled to consider all viewpoints before making decisions. A separate computer search of the same database would produce qualified nominations for legislative representatives and other office holders. The Voting Panel would determine which of the candidates get the position, after comprehensive examination isolated from zealots and vested interests. The voter group would be paid substantially but dismissed after one year.

A decision reached in this way would be far better than the current emotional clamor of indoctrinated voters who decide our fate based on allegiance to political parties and refuse to even listen to alternative opinions. That would actually be more democratic than current balloting processes, more accurately reflect uncontaminated thinking of ordinary citizens, save billions of dollars, reduce ill will that divides America, and eliminate a primary cause of corruption.

Part one of this document reviews original intentions of our Constitution and shows how those intentions have been thwarted by technical and social developments since 1787. Part two explains why a revolution is inevitable if the present system continues and offers incentives for making the proposed changes. Part three outlines a proposed new system using 21st century technology to create the Democratic-Republic our Founding Fathers envisioned but could not produce in the 18th century.

Part One:

Why Revisions Are Needed

Background

There is a revolution coming to the United States. How violent it will be remains to be seen, but casualties are just as dead if they are killed by lynch mobs, artillery, snipers, or ballot boxes. Violence seems highly likely in the pending American Revolution because of the intensity of beliefs involved and the intransigence of those currently in power. Inevitability of revolution reflects the ever-increasing inability of the US Constitution to meet its objectives. The only way to permanently prevent the catastrophe of revolution is to eradicate the ultimate cause of revolutions, and to do that, we must change the Constitution. In particular we must change how our representatives are chosen to halt the drift into disaster. Politicians, left and right, are insisting we must change, but they are not specifying what we should change into.

> **KEY DEFINITIONS**
>
> **Oligarchy** means government by a few. *The Few* may be various groups, alone or in combination.
>
> > **Plutocracy:** the wealthy
> > **Aristocracy:** privileged class or royalty
> > **Theocracy:** religious leaders
> > **Timocracy:** property owners
> > **Bureaucracy:** public employees
> > **Autocracy:** dictatorship
> > **Junta:** military officers, after revolution
>
> **Democracy:** all citizens participate equally in majority-rule decisions.
>
> **Republic:** representatives speak and act for constituents – *The Many*.
>
> **Democratic-Republic:** representatives are chosen by the people they represent.
>
> http://en.wikipedia.org/wiki/Oligarchy

Ultimately, all revolutions can be traced to *The Many* rebelling against exploitation or oppression by *The Few*. Sometimes they are armed military revolutions like the 18th century American Revolution or 20th century armed revolutions in Russia, China, Cuba, or hundreds of lesser ones in the recent centuries. Some revolutions are relatively simple coup d'états rather than pitched battles between armies, but they are nonetheless a populace rising up against oppression, real or perceived.[1] Other social upheavals are often called revolutions, although they do not involve a total overthrow of government. Examples include Industrial Revolutions, Civil Rights Revolutions, Women's Suffrage, Sexual Revolution, Technology Revolutions, and so forth. The Civil Rights Movements of the 1960s involved plenty of violence but not competing military armies. The United States Constitution contains anachronisms that were necessary or wise in the 18th century but do not fit 21st century situations. An example is the Electoral College. It was needed in the 18th century because citizens had no way of knowing candidates from distant colonies, like the eleven men who ran against George Washington in 1788. The Electoral College has no utility in view of modern communications that let voters get well acquainted with candidates 3,000 miles away. It is also notable that Congress has sent thirty-three approved Constitutional Amendments to the States, of which twenty-seven, including the original ten Bill of Rights have been ratified, reflecting points the original authors did not consider or are regarded much differently now than they were in the 18th century. Slavery is an example of

There are innumerable things in our everyday life that would amaze the Forefathers – like aluminum foil and cans. This aluminum coin was minted in 1857 when Aluminum was more expensive than gold. It is the third most abundant element in the earth s crust, after oxygen and silicon, but it is the most abundant metal. Aluminum was used in expensive jewelry before the electrolytic refining process made it abundant and cheap in 1870. Legend has it that Napoleon III had gold dinner cutlery for his ordinary guests, but his VIP guests had the honor of eating dinner with real Aluminum cutlery. Incidentally, Napoleon III s reign ended in1870, but it doesn t seem to be related to his aluminum cutlery.

CARL D. VELEY

something accepted then but not now. There are also issues with some of the amendments. We can only wonder how the Founding Fathers would have defined Freedom of the Press, if they had known about social networking and blogs on the Internet, nationwide broadcasting, or multipage newspapers with millions of readers. The third amendment deals with compulsory quartering of troops in peacetime. That was a major issue leading up to the revolution but has not been an important issue since before the Civil War.

Then there is the evolution of the economy and other civic factors. For example the Seventh Amendment to the US Constitution states:

> *In suits at common law, where the value in controversy shall exceed twenty dollars, the right of trial by jury shall be preserved, and no fact tried by a jury, shall be otherwise reexamined in any court of the United States, than according to the rules of the common law.*

Suppose you argue with your neighbor over $50 worth of fence repairs. The 7th Amendment clearly guarantees you the right to demand a jury trial costing thousands of 21st century dollars, but you can be sure that's not going to happen. That amendment will be interpreted according to its 1787 intent, not its verbatim wording in 21st century language. Note also that the 7th Amendment could be construed as prohibiting appeals courts, but that has not been the prevailing interpretation.

We must consider 18th century colonial life to understand the Constitution's authors and adapt their intentions to the technical and social changes since that time. It is the Supreme Court's job to determine what the Constitution's authors had in mind and adapt the many anachronisms to contemporary language and technology.

Colonial Life – Technology

Life was hard in the American colonies in the late 18th century. There was no indoor plumbing and often no ready source of water for firefighting. Mobile steam engines, high-pressure pumps and hoses had not yet been developed, so firefighting was mostly just volunteers in bucket brigades. Rats, mice, and other vermin were abundant, and there was no chemical defense against termites. Log cabins had a short life expectancy on the frontiers, and brick or stone houses were expensive.

Bacteria were discovered in 1670 but were not widely understood in 1787, and viruses were not discovered until 1892, a century later. There were no antibiotics, vaccinations, or anesthesia in the 18th century. Diseases were rampant, including typhoid, diphtheria, tetanus, cholera, rabies, smallpox, and polio. Relatively minor wounds or injuries often contracted serious infections, surgery was dreadfully painful or impossible, infant mortality was about 25% in the colonies or 40% worldwide, and life expectancy was in the range of thirty to forty years. The first vaccine, preventing smallpox, appeared in 1796 but was not widely available until the early 19th century, and aspirin was first made in 1897.

Colonials would have been amazed by a flashlight because batteries were a laboratory curiosity in 1800 and not available in useful form until after the American Civil War. Matches that could be ignited by friction came along in 1826. Colonials started a fire with flint and steel, but steel was expensive and mostly only used for knives, swords, and armor. It only became feasible for large items, like railroad rails, in 1856 when the Bessemer process was developed in England. The Eiffel tower was the first demonstration of the suitability of steel for high-rise construction. That was a century after the Constitution was adopted.

It was difficult to preserve and store food for the winter. Food canning in glass jars was being developed in France for Napoleon's army but did not reach America until the early 19th century.[2] Dairy products were first pasteurized in the mid-19th century.

Logistics were slow and unreliable because there were no railroads, no paved highways, and nothing faster than horse drawn wagons for moving freight overland. Business was local because it was impractical to market goods more than a few miles from where they were produced. There were no electric motors, steam or gasoline engines, cotton gins, or motorized farm machinery. There were no assembly line factories because precision-made interchangeable parts were not available. Candles were a major night light source because oil made from coal was smoky, kerosene made from crude oil was not yet available, and whale oil was expensive. The Spinning Jenny was just beginning the transformation of spinning thread from slow "cottage industries" to high volume textile factories.

There were no telephones, telegraphs, or any instant communication method with greater range than a church bell, and it might take days to learn of things that happened just twenty miles away. That made emergency responses slow and limited to local resources. Everyone was expected to participate in firefighting and assist during emergencies, but there were few full-time public employees.

All governments were oligarchies in the 18th century and effectively remain so today. The sidebar lists the major types, but a search of the Internet produces a list[3] of 114 words ending in '…cracy' with a web page devoted to each one. Exhaustively studying the entire list might be a good cure for insomnia, but readers are advised to review Kakistocracy[4] and perhaps a few others to better understand contemporary political matters.

EXCERPT FROM ORDERS GIVEN TO BRITISH COMMANDER, APRIL 18, 1775 IN BOSTON, MASSACHUSETTS COLONY

"Having received intelligence, that a quantity of Ammunition, Provisions, Artillery, Tents and small Arms, have been collected at Concord, for the Avowed Purpose of raising and supporting a Rebellion against His Majesty, you will March with a Corps of Grenadiers and Light Infantry, put under your Command, with the utmost expedition and Secrecy to Concord, where you will seize and distroy [sic] all Artillery, Ammunition, Provisions, Tents, Small Arms, and all Military Stores whatever. **But you will take care that the Soldiers do not plunder the Inhabitants, or hurt private property.**" [Emphasis added]

https://teachingamericanhistory.org/library/document/orders-from-general-thomas-gage-to-lieut-colonel-smith-10th-regiment-foot/

Rulers (Autocrats) in the 18th century went by different names, King, Kaiser, Emperor, Sultan, Tsar, or whatever, but it amounted to the same thing, various forms of oligarchy, all with a heavy dose of theocracy. Britain had a parliament that passed laws, but King George III and his cronies routinely ignored Parliament and Britain functioned as an oligarchy. The colonials yearned for a government with ordinary people controlling their own destiny by deciding the laws that governed them, but such a system was not in place anywhere in the world. Authors of the USA Constitution were striving to create one. They did amazingly well, considering what was known in the 18th century, but knowledge and experience have expanded and advanced in ways that could not have been foreseen.

There are many outmoded features of the Constitution. One of the most troublesome is the Second Amendment. It deserves special consideration to understand why the Constitution desperately needs to be updated.

Colonial Militias

Security was a major problem for pioneering colonials, especially those in rural or isolated communities. The longest-range call for help was a church bell whose range and direction depended on the wind. They had to rely on local volunteers in emergencies such as fires or criminal attacks. For this purpose, the colonials had militias – loosely organized, volunteer, self-trained, part-time, locally controlled, military units. They also performed police functions, but they were basically military, primarily concerned with defense – Indian attacks in the northern colonies and slave uprisings in the southern colonies. They were subject to callup by the States in time of actual war. These militias were more like vigilantes or a posse than regular army, but they were important to communities, large or small, because outside help was slow or unavailable.[5]

The opening battle of the American revolution was on the 19th of April 1775. The British were concerned about the large militias of Concord and Lexington and sent soldiers to seize their armories.[6] That would leave colonials with no means of defense against criminal raiders and force them to depend on the slow and very unreliable British army.

A widespread contemporary belief holds that the British soldiers were attempting to seize privately owned guns when Paul Revere and his associated riders sounded the alarm and started the first battle of the Revolutionary War. The sidebar is the first paragraph of orders issued by General Thomas Gage to Lieutenant Colonel Smith that defined the British mission that day and specifically forbid seizing privately owned weapons. They were only after the armories and military supplies for the militias.

The Founding Fathers' concept of militias is evident in the Articles of Confederation that defined the initial USA government in 1781 but were replaced by the present Constitution in 1788. Confederation Article 6 required the States to maintain a militia for the common defense but subject to callup by the Federal Government in the event of war. Officers ranked captain and below were set by State legislatures.

This in effect defined what we call today a National Guard and reflected Colonial fear of a central government raiding their armories, neutralizing their militias and crippling their security. The second amendment of the present Constitution refers to that sort of military militia and has nothing to do with individuals owning firearms. In 1787, stating that a frontiersman had a right to own a gun would have been as nonsensical as saying a farmer had a right to own a cow or plant crops. Of course he did, and of course he had a right to protect his livestock from predators and his family from marauders. But it would not have made sense in 1787 to declare an individual had a right to assemble firepower greater than the existing State Militias. Rural colonials often had "fowling pieces" that today would be called shotguns – OK for hunting but not suited for warfare. In the event of a call to report for militia duty, it did not make sense for a volunteer to waste time dashing home to pick up an unsuitable weapon, so communities kept armories where the volunteers could be supplied, at public expense, with a suitable weapon, ammunition, and supplies. Additionally the armories had military supplies, such as tents, cannons, food, and things needed for a military excursion but not for daily life.

The second amendment was intended to protect the right of autonomous groups, from small communities to entire States, to maintain armories for the militias they relied on for security. This is largely irrelevant in 21st century language where security is provided by well-regulated police and national guard units instead of vigilantes that can become lynch mobs. The Founding Fathers sought to prevent a strong central government from consolidating power and taking over security by disarming militias, as the British army was attempting to do when their raids on Concord and Lexington armories precipitated the Revolutionary War.[6] That is why the second amendment reads:

> *A well-regulated Militia, being necessary to the security of a free State,*
> *the right of the people to keep and bear Arms, shall not be infringed.*

The colonials had never known a nation other than an all-powerful oligarchy, and to them, "the people" meant everyone else in the nation, other than the rulers. When the Preamble says, *"We the people..."* it is referring to "people" as *The Many* or the whole of society. When Lincoln, in the Gettysburg Address a century later, said, "...Government of the people, by the people, and for the people..." he was not suggesting that individual citizens should govern only themselves. He was describing the Constitution's intention – laws made by *The Many* through representatives.

Authors of the Constitution could not imagine cars, airplanes, television, or 20th century weapons. A dozen men with AR-15s and ammunition could easily have defeated 1,500 British at the 1775 battles of Lexington and Concord. The Founding Fathers would never have agreed that one man should have the firepower of several 18th century brigades, like Stephen Paddock did on October 1st, 2017 in Las Vegas. He opened fire on concert goers,

> **INCULCATION**
>
> Inculcation is a method of instilling ideas by repetition of a message that may or may not be factual. When people hear or see an advertisement hundreds of times, they tend to accept it as true, even if the claim is clearly false. The phenomenon is exploited via advertising for commercial marketing and for political purposes. Political campaigns are mostly indoctrination by inculcation.

killing fifty-eight and wounding 413, with the ensuing panic raising the injury total to 869. That one man with 21st century arms and ammunition could easily have overpowered State Militias in 1787 and could have won any battle of the revolutionary war, single-handed. Allowing individuals to possess automatic weapons gives them the killing power of a large, undisciplined, and unregulated 1787 militia and creates thousands of them across the country, some in the hands of psychopaths like Stephen Paddock. No reasonable person can claim that was the intent of the Constitution's authors.

It is time to revisit the Constitution and its Amendments and restate the Authors' intentions in light of technical and social developments and in 21st century language.

Colonial Life – Social and Political

There were major social issues in 1787 in addition to lacking devices, conveniences, and comforts we consider essential in modern times. Slaves, indentured servants, and women were treated as property and denied equal status with white, Anglo-Saxon, Protestant men. Public schooling was not universal, and illiterate adult citizens were frequently cheated and exploited. Colonials had advantages over the serfs of medieval Europe, but they were still subjects of the English King who demanded heavy taxes, in part to pay for the French and Indian War. Taxation without representation was a major complaint in the colonies, as it is now for residents of Washington DC.

The Revolutionary War effectively ended in 1781 when Washington defeated Cornwallis at Yorktown, but it did not officially end until the Treaty of Paris was signed in 1783. The new nation, The United States of America, was formed in 1781 under the Articles of Confederation. The Articles featured strong State governments loosely linked by a weak Federal government, reflecting colonial fear of strong central governments and a belief that personal liberty required local autonomy. It was a disaster, with States issuing their own money, squabbling among themselves, evading Federal taxes, and even making separate treaties with other countries. It quickly became obvious that the States could not be truly united without a strong central government.

A constitutional convention was called in 1787 with the objective of defining a strong central government that would:

> Standardize and unify common interests, such as postal services, interstate commerce, national security, foreign treaties, judicial systems, money, and so forth.

> Preserve local autonomy when possible.

> Assure personal liberty.

> Resist takeovers by tyrants or oligarchies.

It was believed that representatives, fairly chosen, would empower *The Many* and create legislation likely to benefit common people without being anarchy. However, a Republic empowers a small group of representatives and thus forms *A Few* that effectively becomes an oligarchy, with potential for benefiting themselves and exploiting *The Many*. Authors of the Constitution were themselves an oligarchy of affluent colonials, but at most, they were only a generation or two away from what would today be called working class immigrants. They had a much better understanding of working class needs and problems than the oligarchs of England. In the 1780s, subsistence farmers, tradesmen, and shopkeepers could not afford to be away from home for weeks at a time, paying travel expenses, and therefore they did not participate in drafting the Constitution. Fortunately for them, and for all Americans since, the Constitution authors were aware of the tendency for avarice to change governments into oligarchies and recognized their need to counter that tendency.

The principle features of the Constitution intended to slow or prevent oligarchies are term limits and checks and balances that divide power. Limiting terms to two years in the House and six years in the Senate gave voters an opportunity to remove anyone abusing their power, but it also raised the cost of campaigning. That was not a major issue in 1787 because campaigning was not so costly and it was not foreseen that campaigns would become incredibly expensive, be a major cause of corruption, and assure the rise of a plutocratic oligarchy.

The Constitution's authors had these principles in mind:

- People in power tend to enact laws beneficial to themselves.

- The only way to assure laws that truly benefit ordinary people is to have ordinary people make the laws.

- Those in power tend to legislate in ways that consolidate and expand their power.

- Checks and balances are needed to distribute power and prevent tyranny.

- Given accurate information, ordinary people are just as intelligent as aristocrats and are equally capable of thoughtful debate and sound conclusions.

- Legislation should be passed after rational discussion and careful consideration and not in the heat of transient passion following a momentous event.

- ➤ Laws and regulations should be fair and just, protecting human rights for all citizens.

- ➤ Pure Democracy requires the entire population to vote on every minor issue and is therefore unworkable, except in very small groups.

- ➤ In the long-run, a Democratic-Republic will only work if representatives truly represent *The Many* and are not selected by an oligarchy or allowed to become an oligarchy themselves.

"Power tends to corrupt; absolute power. corrupts absolutely."

This often-quoted statement by Lord Acton, a British historian, came about a century after the USA Constitution was created, but the phenomenon was well-known to the Founding Fathers. The purpose of a three-part Government is checks and balances to prevent individuals or oligarchies from gaining power that will inevitably be abused.

There are snags to all majority rule systems. For example, the same year the USA Constitution was ratified, 1789, the French Revolution began. It put Robespierre in power, and his short but extremely violent reign enacted vengeance for *The Many*, but they were poor people enraged by centuries of suppression and exploitation. His mob rules sent royalty, wealthy people, and educated leaders to the guillotine for two years before Robespierre, too, was beheaded. Blood flowed in the streets of Paris and the country was in chaos, making an opportunity for an organizer like Napoleon to seize control.

Poor people were by far the majority, but that didn't mean they were compassionate or qualified to govern. The French Revolution, like all revolutions, was soon taken over by an oligarchy. Examples of this phenomenon from the 20th century are the Russian and Chinese revolutions that were intended to favor common people but in fact established an oligarchy of party officials that quickly became corrupt and oppressed rather than advanced common people. The oligarchy put in place by the American Revolution has developed more slowly, but it is real and insidiously destructive.

The 1787 challenge was how to put *The Many* in charge without empowering malevolent, unqualified, self-serving, or vindictive masses. A Democratic-Republic was favored in 1787 and still is today, with communities, cities, counties, and States choosing representatives by voting and majority rules. There were problems: 1) defining who can vote, 2) potential for manipulation of voters' opinions and sentiments via communication methods not possible in the 18th century, 3) susceptibility of the voting process to the corrupting influence of wealth and voter indoctrinations. (See 'Inculcations' sidebar.)

Defining Who Can Vote

Framers of the Constitution assumed George Washington would run unopposed, but in fact, there were twelve Presidential candidates in 1788. That made voting more complex than expected and the States, unaccustomed to holding elections, all handled balloting differently.[7]

Voter turnout was low in the Presidential election of 1788, with a single digit percentage of the adult population casting a ballot, although voting occurred over two weeks, not one day. Two States, North Carolina and Rhode Island, did not vote because they had not yet ratified the Constitution, New York's Legislature did not choose their Electors on time, and some states voted directly for the candidates while others only voted for their delegates to the Electoral College. Free black men could vote in four States, (Virginia,

Pennsylvania, New Jersey, and North Carolina) and women could vote in New Jersey until 1807. Most States allowed only tax-paying, white, male property owners to vote, (about 6% of the population) and a few directly violated the new Constitution with religious tests for voters.

It was not until 1803 that the Supreme Court declared the Constitution was actual law and not just a statement of principle, meaning the courts could strike down laws that violated the Constitution. It was 1868, after the Civil War, when the 14th Amendment definitively established that State laws must abide by the Constitution and could not violate Federal law.[8]

Manipulating Voters' Opinions

Advertising was primitive in the 18th century and mostly limited to local announcements. The rudimentary opinion-molding advertising of the 18th century was primarily posters and single-page flyers hand-printed and distributed locally. A political activist of the time, Paul Revere, better known for his midnight ride calling militias to the battle of Concord, made and distributed ads that were not rigorously factual but effective in molding opinions.[9] It was not until printing advances made ads more successful, and better transportation made wide distribution feasible that advertising and political campaigns developed on a national scale.

After the civil war, a demand grew rapidly for experts in creating brief, punchy slogans, with celebrity endorsements and art to make ads highly effective in manipulating public opinion or influencing behavior.

Have you noticed watches in ads are always set at 10:10? That tells us the watch is "happy" without saying so. The information is the time is 10:10 but the message is "This watch will make you happy because it is happy." Advertising experts know how to present their information to subliminally transmit the message they want. Political experts use advertising methods to transmit messages that may or may not be factual but effectively mold opinions. (Watches are not actually happy or sad.)

      CARL D. VELEY

The ads' effectiveness in molding opinions has been demonstrated many times, with an example coming in the 20th century when court cases established that tobacco companies targeted ads to attract teen customers.

Some people insist they are not influenced by advertising, but that is simply not true. All are influenced, but some are more easily inculcated than others. The phenomenon is exploited for political purposes, with advertising experts creating images that may or may not be ethical or truthful but are powerful utilizations of verbal and non-verbal communication in opinion molding.

Printed ads, widely distributed, are effective and expensive, but television ads are even more effective and expensive. Contemporary candidates for Federal office cannot expect to win an election without spending millions on TV ads, much more than any "ordinary" person can afford. Candidates need money from people who expect something to happen in return for their contribution. Candidates and parties raise huge sums by collecting small donations from millions of people, but a single million-dollar donor has far more influence than 100,000 donors giving $10 each. Small donors' money is allocated by a limited number of party officials who, together with the megadonors, become a plutocracy, an oligarchy the Constitution sought to prevent.

Tobacco companies used ads featuring celebrities or carefully crafted cartoon characters (like Joe Camel) to convince people, particularly teens, that smoking was "cool". Politicians use ad techniques to appear "cool" and to demonize opponents.

Truth in advertising is enforced by the Federal Trade Commission established in 1914. Before then advertising was notoriously deceptive. An example was an ad that offered an insect killer guaranteed to kill all types of insect pests. When the customer received the product, it was two wooden blocks labeled "A" and "B" with instructions, "Place insect on block A and strike with block B." True? Yes, technically. Deceptive? Very. Legal? At the time, yes but not after 1914. Dishonest or misleading political ads are harder to prove or prevent.

There were no political parties in 1788, but voters were generally split into Federalists, those favoring strong central government, and Anti-Federalists, who favored autonomous State and local governments. Candidates for office had no allegiance to a political party and essentially ran as independents. Candidates for President did not choose a running mate and the runner-up for President became Vice President. Problems with that were quickly noted and the 12th Amendment changed to the present system in 1804.

Technical and Social Factors Affecting Voting

The 19th century saw the USA expand to the Pacific coast via the Louisiana Purchase, war with Mexico, and the Alaska purchase.[10] The USA also fought a civil war, experienced the industrial revolution, ended slavery, and absorbed a flood of immigrants. Major inventions included the cotton gin, sewing machine, steel plow, reaper, multi-shot cartridge-loaded rifles and pistols, factories utilizing interchangeable parts and assembly lines, public distribution of electricity, and inexpensive steel making, along with development of railroads, telegraphs, and the first oil well drilled in 1859 that put kerosene on the market and led to the gasoline engine and "horseless carriages."

Men, including Andrew Carnegie, Andrew Mellon, Henry Ford, J.P. Morgan, and J.D. Rockefeller (called "Captains of Industry" by supporters and "Robber Barons" by their detractors), created trusts and monopolies that greatly influenced candidates and legislation. Willian Randolph Hearst and Joseph Pulitzer created "yellow journalism" that used hyperbole, melodrama, and distortion to inaccurately influence voters.[11] These men were oligarchs. Their power did not involve directly issuing laws; it came from using critical industries and services to effectively hold politicians and ordinary citizens in bondage[12] by determining who became legislators and by demanding favorable regulations. This was accomplished in large part by manipulating voters' opinions through unscrupulous advertising.

Politicians *Need* Enemies

Events can be ranked in the familiar bell-shape curve, from unusually bad, to normal, to unusually good. The majority will be "normal" and it is not necessary to do anything special in response. When an event is unusually good, there may be cause for celebration but no need for a corrective action. We only feel a need for action when something unusually bad happens or threatens to happen. It follows that politicians' calls for action will always be about correcting something that is causing harm or soon will be. They cannot offer "cures" for something normal or beneficial, and the greater the potential harm, the greater the need for corrective or defensive action. Inevitably political messages will overstate potential harm in order to create or amplify a sense of urgency for their proposed action – voting for a certain candidate or proposition. It's a perfect opportunity for the inculcating power of ads repeated hundreds of times to promote viewpoints, demonize opponents, and generally indoctrinate voters.

Americans shared a common enemy during forty years of Cold War – Communism. Few people could accurately define Communism but were nonetheless passionately opposed to it and considered it a major threat. Politicians would argue over who was best qualified to combat it, but there was agreement that it was indeed an enemy needing action. When the Communism threat went away, a new enemy was needed, or politicians would have no basis for a call for action. Candidates identified a problem, exaggerated it as much as possible, and blamed it on their opposition. The parties stopped considering *Them* as adversaries seeking the same goals as *Us* but holding differing

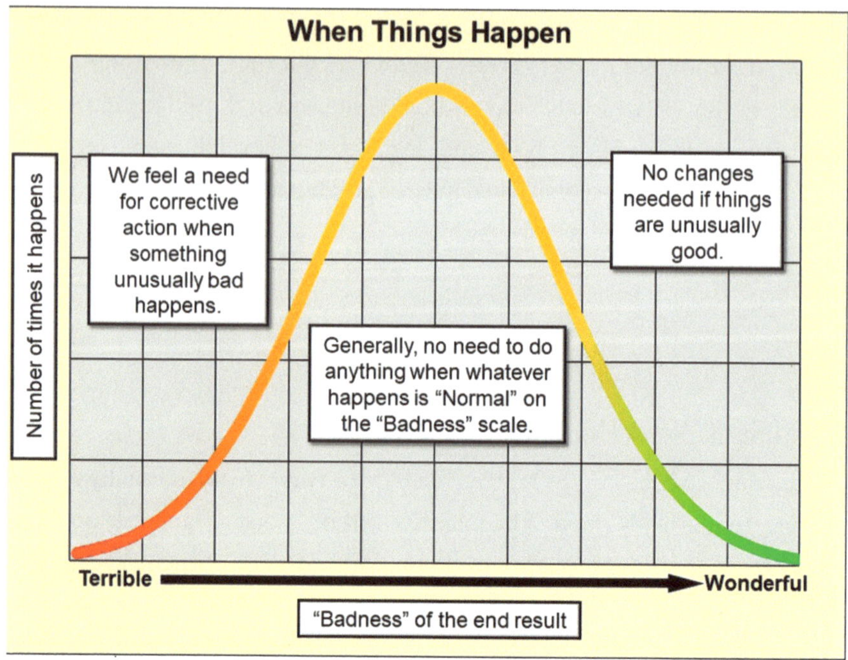

FIGURE 1 *Action is needed to correct things that are bad or to prevent things from going bad. Political campaigns are a call for action, ("Vote for me") and always reduce to identifying something bad and claiming to be better able to correct it than the opponent.*

opinions on the best way to achieve those goals. We stopped seeing each other as debate opponents who must be argued with and started seeing each other as mortal enemies who must be *destroyed*. The result has been ratcheting up demonization and polarizing hatred that stifles debate and smothers any hope for a functioning Republic.

Faith-Based Reasoning

The word *faith* means, *"Accepting something as true, in the absence of proof."* It is not limited to religious assumptions or dogma, and it is not always wrong. For example you might have faith that someone is honest and would never steal.

     CARL D. VELEY

That cannot be proved. It may be possible to prove they *did* do something dishonest, but it is impossible to prove what someone *would not do*. That doesn't mean your faith is wrong or misplaced, it simply means it cannot be proved.

All human conflicts, from two-person quarrels to World Wars, result from points of faith. There are never fights over chemistry, mathematics, physics, or anything that can be proved. We only fight over things that can NOT be proved. We fight over value judgements, assumptions, assertions, subjective claims, beliefs, religion, and other points of faith, but nobody fights over things that can be proved. This is the danger of faith-based reasoning, it is the ultimate root of all human conflict.

Problems develop when people ignore or reject observations or logic and cling to their faith. An extreme example would be devoutly religious people who reject vaccines or medicine of any form and rely completely on divine providence to protect health of themselves and their children. Another example would be parents so strongly believing their son's claim of innocence that they reject video showing him shoplifting. A more insidious and more harmful example occurs when people reason: A) I am *good because* my religious beliefs are thus-and-so, B) You do not believe thus-and-so, therefore, C) you are *not good*. People prone to faith-based reasoning accept something as true simply because a trusted authority says it is true, or it coincides

> **ATHEISM**
>
> Everyone believes there is such a thing as love but find it hard to explain. A theistic explanation holds that an invisible personality named Cupid shoots invisible magic arrows into people's hearts. Non-theists (atheists) scoff at this assumption and insist the biological and psychological elements of love may not be fully understood, but they are totally certain that love does NOT involve super-natural, omnipotent personalities named Cupid, Eros, Aphrodite, Venus, or whatever.
>
> Everyone agrees there is an ultimate reality – that for which there is no explanation and no origin. Theists assume it is a personality with a combination of human characteristics and super-natural powers. Atheists dispute the nature of ultimate reality but they do not doubt its existence. They insist it is not a personality. Atheists insist gods, mono theistic or poly theistic, are personalities created by theists to explain things they cannot otherwise understand.

with their pre-existing beliefs. This phenomenon is particularly harmful in politics, when voters have become so indoctrinated by their Party's assertions that they reflexively reject anything and everything from the opposition Party, regardless of evidence or logic. They have excessive faith in their leaders and will not, or cannot, objectively consider facts that contradict their beliefs.

Teaching Voters to Hate

Children are not born hating and must learn it somehow. But if an adult told a child, "Hate that person!" it would be ineffective because hatred cannot be taught directly. Instead adults teach children that "we" are superior and peaceful, while "they" are inferior and dangerous. Hatred is a *consequence* of teaching, not a subject matter to be taught. Hatred is the ugly child of Scorn and Fear, and that is what adults teach, often with little or no factual evidence. The distinction between *us* and *them* is commonly made on the basis of race, language, religion, gender, sexual orientation, or nationality, but it can also be based on political affiliations. Adults typically do not realize they are teaching hatred – they

POLITICS OF FEAR

Ultimately, we only attack people we hate, and that means we fear them and consider them inferior. Political campaigns concentrate on creating fear of the opposition candidate and his or her platform, knowing that voters are more likely to vote against someone they hate than they are to vote for someone they admire.

Contrast that with foreign policy. We never consider going to war with a country we consider inferior, unless we are also afraid they will cause harm to us or our friends. Politicians who generate fear to destroy their opponents also work to make other countries fear us. That was the objective of 40 years of Cold War and arms race, not to mention wars in Korea and Vietnam. We suffer attacks if others consider us inferior and fear our influence on their future. Flexing our military muscle doesn't change likelihood of attack but it changes method of attack, from a military Pearl Harbor to a terrorist 9/11.

believe they are protecting children by alerting them to danger and combatting the perceived enemy.

An inculcation of political messages insisting the opposition is both stupid and dangerous creates hatred.

Politicians seldom say, "Our opponents believe thus-and-so will improve the situation, but it will really make the situation worse, and here is the reason why." Instead politicians use emotion-laden terms, "Our opponents want to *ruin* America, *crush* our freedom, *destroy* our economy by methodical, and *deliberate oppression* of common people like us." We tend to assail opponents' character rather than dispute their assumptions. We counter their faith-based arguments with our own faith-based arguments and ignore or discredit arguments based on logic and reason. Such passionate language creates hatred, based on inaccurate assumptions and beliefs. Americans have experienced increasing inculcation since political parties first organized. We hate each other based on our politics, and hatred is growing as political messages are ever more malicious and belligerent. We are becoming steadily less willing to examine our own beliefs and assumptions, and ever less willing to compromise.

The net effect of campaign tactics is that elections no longer determine the will of Americans, they determine the prevailing belief of *indoctrinated* Americans, and that's a subtle but important difference. Voters who are not obsessed with some issue and have not been inculcated are less concerned about who wins, and they tend to abstain from voting. People are less motivated to vote *for* someone they like than they are to vote *against* someone they hate, and if they don't hate a candidate, there's a good chance they will think it doesn't matter who wins and they simply won't vote. This phenomenon removes rational thought from the decision-making process. Winners are indoctrinated one way, while losers are indoctrinated another way and may not accept defeat gracefully.

Political experts predict election winners based on how much money the candidates raise because that determines ability to repetitively broadcast ads generating scorn and fear of the opposition through inculcation. It's a sad commentary on American politics that those campaigns most likely to win are the ones most effective in creating hatred and billions of dollars are spent for that purpose, whether consciously or not.

Who Seeks Office

High political office is not attractive for ordinary people. Campaigning is hard work, requires total commitment, long hours, time away from home and family, and even if successful, it leads to a difficult job that creates numerous personal enemies. People most likely to want such a job are those who are zealous about some controversial subject, have a strong conviction that opposing opinions and members of the other party are stupid and dangerous (meaning they are motivated by hate, as herein defined), and firmly believe their superior intellect can "protect" misguided voters by enacting legislation in

Campaigning for elective office is inevitably acrimonious, and the candidate most likely to win is the one most effective in demonizing opponents. Elections are divisive and are a major inhibitor to an essential element of Democracy – Loyal Opposition. Majority Rule cannot endure unless those holding minority opinions remain loyal despite losing the vote.

line with the candidate's beliefs. There is a tendency to view "leadership" as leading the constituents where the candidate wants to go rather than leading them where they want to go. The zealotry that wins support from indoctrinated voters and financial backers inhibits elected representatives from rationally debating and seeking the best problem solutions, irrespective of party platforms.

It follows that candidates for high office are not, and probably cannot become, truly representative of non-indoctrinated, thoughtful, ordinary citizens. They are highly likely to be, or soon become, exactly the sort of people the Constitution authors sought to exclude from law-making authority. It's high time we review our process for selecting people who make our laws, and also review the process by which those rules are made.

Ideally a republic reaches the same conclusions a democracy would reach because the representatives think the same as the whole group. In review this does not currently happen for these reasons:

- ➤ Representatives typically are not ordinary people.

  - ➤ Those who seek office tend to be heavily inculcated and zealous about a controversial issue. Their obsessions attract financial support but inhibit them from rationally considering alternative views.

  - ➤ Campaigning is extremely expensive and feasible only for people who are personally wealthy or willing to make commitments to wealthy vested interests. People with those characteristics are not representatives of "ordinary people."

- ➤ Voters have been so heavily inculcated by political messages that they will not, or cannot, evaluate candidates dispassionately when casting their ballots.

- ➤ Successful candidates have also been so heavily inculcated that they cannot rationally consider alternative viewpoints or arguments when making decisions.

- ➤ Campaigns are so expensive that corruption is inevitable, and representatives will abandon needs of their constituents to further interests of their financial benefactors.

- ➤ Elected officials are indebted to political parties for campaign assistance and focus on party goals at the expense of their constituents' wishes or even their own conscience.

- ➤ When money controls who gets elected and what laws are passed, the republic has become a plutocracy, an oligarchy that the Constitution was intended to prevent.

- ➤ The Speaker of the House and the Senate Majority Leader control what legislation is considered, creating another form of oligarchy that precludes a true democratic-republic.

> Perhaps the greatest flaw in the present system is the lack of real deliberation. Routine sessions in Congress consist of a member reading a speech into the record in front of an almost empty chamber. Few, if any, other members are even listening to what is being said. There is no real debate.

> Pressure to conform to party agendas is a major obstacle to thoughtful deliberation, and even if an "ordinary" citizen reaches congress, his or her objectivity is suppressed by party officials.

> The cost of holding elections is truly staggering.[13]

> Political party expenses and the costs of campaigning ultimately are paid by people who expect a particular outcome as a return on their investment.

> Judges, all the way to Supreme Court justices, are chosen based on their political bias, not the impartiality that should be their dominant characteristic.

> Gerrymandering is a direct assault on Democracy, deliberately designed to dilute the impact of certain voters and thus distort the will of the people.

The republic intended by the Constitution does not exist, and maybe it never did. Rules devised in 1778 cannot be expected to solve 21st century problems blocking a democratic-republic. That is still the fairest form of government provided the law-making is done by people who are truly representative of all the governed, and deliberate honestly, free from fanatical or obsessive pressures and indoctrination. Currently the USA is ruled by an oligarchy of zealous plutocrats and autocrats. We need a process to select representatives that is immune to the corruption of dark money, uncompromising political zealots, autocratic political leadership, and inculcating partisan campaigns.

Part Two:

The Coming Revolution

The Oligarchy Cycle

In 1911. Robert Michels published a book titled *Political Parties*. His "Iron Law of Oligarchy" held that necessary division of labor in any large organization inevitably leads to a ruling class or oligarchy.[14] Someone must make rules for others to follow. The rule makers, being human, tend to overrate their own importance, tend to make rules (laws) that are beneficial to themselves, and are strongly concerned with consolidating and expanding their own power. Michels postulated that all large organizations, including governments, are controlled by oligarchies. This was not an entirely new concept. In the fourth century BCE, the Athenians combatted this phenomenon by drawing lots to select qualified people for civic duties and political responsibilities.

People who seek rule-making power tend to have these general characteristics:

➤ They have a strong, sometimes overpowering, ego – including a high opinion of their own intelligence and an intense faith in their personal assumptions.

➤ They often believe that it is usually bad to have someone in power for a long time, but in their personal case, they should remain in power as long as they are physically able, to maximize their contribution to the betterment of society.

➤ They often believe their rise to power was the work of divine providence and those who oppose them are guided by the forces of evil.

➤ They assume they have a right, or an actual obligation, to expand their power and weaken the ability of citizens to resist or oppose their decisions.

As oligarchies increase their power, they ratchet up oppression until finally *The Many* revolt and set up a new government that either begins as, or soon becomes, another oligarchy, in a ceaseless political cycle. If this is true, no government is eternal, and neither is any large corporation.[15] Support for this hypothesis is that there are very few large companies more than 200-years-old, in part because ruling oligarchs (aka Top Managers) tend to overrate their own importance and increase their personal rewards far beyond their true worth. It's ultimately death by oligarchy for any large organization, including the government of The United States of America. The question is not "Will it happen?" but "When will it happen, and how violent will it be?" The answers may come sooner than expected.

Revolutions, rebellions, coups, and uprisings are more common than people realize.[16] Ask a random stranger when the last revolution occurred in the USA, and a likely answer will be the 18th century war for independence. Some might say the Civil War and fewer will say the Civil Rights Movement of the 1960s or the revolt against the Vietnam War in the 1970s. Hardly anyone will mention the Battle of Blair Mountain, the largest armed uprising in US history outside the civil war.[17] It happened in August of 1921 and involved thousands of West Virginia coal miners rebelling against mine owners and authorities. Then there was the Ten Days War in Colorado with miners using dynamite and rifles against machine guns, cannon, and aircraft used by the Colorado National Guard, private detective agencies and a mine company owned by J.D. Rockefeller. That one happened in 1914. Like all rebellions and revolutions, there was a long-standing pattern of exploitation that created a strong resentment and then an event that precipitated rebellion. The precipitating event of the Ten Days War was the Ludlow Massacre.[18]

At what point will *The Many*, nationally, no longer tolerate being exploited and rebel? There doesn't seem to be a scientific method to answer that, but it is a combination of factors. First, there is an underlying frustration or resentment and then there must be a triggering event or situation. If a high precision measure of exploitation existed, it still would not predict when oppression will become so severe that a triggering incident will be enough to incite a revolution.

     CARL D. VELEY

One of the sources of class discontent is the distribution of wealth. It is possible to quantitatively measure wealth disparity, but it is not possible to pinpoint when the disparity will be severe enough to cause a revolution.

Measuring Exploitation

The French Revolution began with the storming of the Bastille on July 14th, 1789. Apparently the French aristocracy was surprised by how strongly they were hated by *The Many*. The wealthy oligarchs believed their exalted social status and mind-boggling wealth were their divine right. They honestly believed they were superior to the "rabble," or as Marx called them, the proletariat. Whether or not Marie Antionette actually made her infamous "Let them eat cake" comment, it is a good illustration of how ignorant the wealthy were about the reality that would soon overwhelm them. We might wonder if our 21st century oligarchs are likewise unaware of how close they are to revolution and the rising danger to themselves personally.

Figure 2 shows the wealthiest 20% of Americans have more collective wealth than the other 80% of the population combined. This condition has prevailed for a long time and is getting even more disparate. Exploitation is increasing and resentment is inevitably increasing, although largely out of sight.

Figures 3 and 4 show the rich get richer and the poor get poorer, even when limiting the discussion to the very wealthy. It seems unlikely that Americans who are dissatisfied with wealth in the hundreds of millions and strive for billions through exploitation realize how similar their situation is to that of the French aristocracy in 1780. There is no point in lamenting the situation, it is human nature, and eliminating it would require eradicating the human species. If we cannot eliminate greed, we must either accept it and just live with it, or we must develop political systems that suppress it or compensate in some way. That is where this discussion is headed.

Some wealth disparity is good and desirable, but as exploitation becomes excessive, it is oppression of *The Many* by *The Few*, and as oppression increases, so does the probability of revolution. But just what is "excessive?" We don't have complete economic data for France in 1788 or Russia in 1916 or China in 1948, and there are multiple, complex factors that lead to revolutions, but wealth disparity is an important indicator of resentment. Disparities along racial, ethnic, or class groupings is a common cause of increasing resentment that turns into desperation and revolution when some triggering event occurs.

In a theoretical Utopian society, everyone would be equal. They would all live in comfort, but nobody would have an income greater than that of anyone else, and any 20% of the population would have 20% of the total income. There would be no "top" or "bottom" income because all would be the same, and in this imaginary society, *everyone would be happy with equality*. In practice this is a bad idea because people are not all the same and will never be happy to totally equal wealth. Some people are more industrious, more curious, more

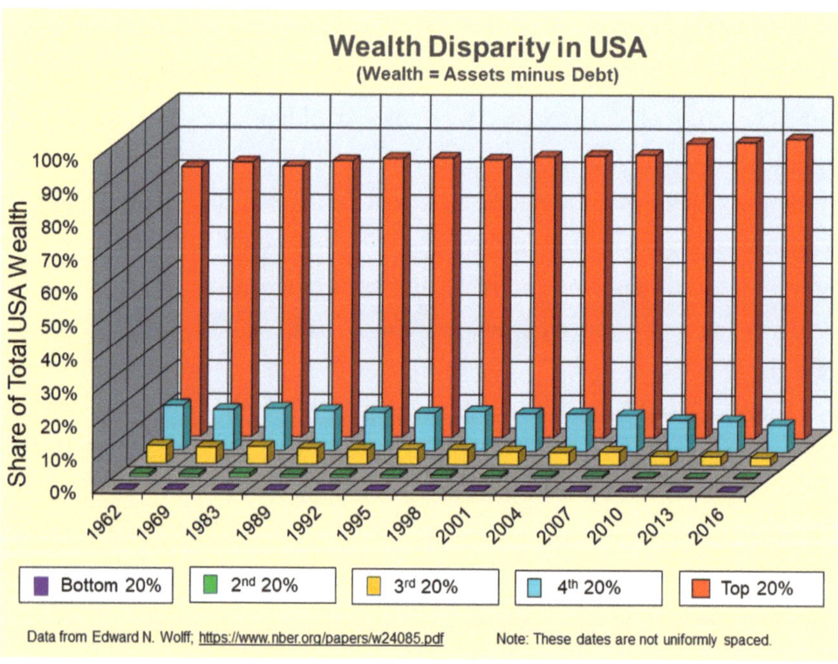

FIGURE 2 *The top 20% of Americans have far more wealth than the other 80%. It is not quantitatively clear how this disparity compares to the disparity in France, Russia, or China, just before their revolutions, but it is clear that disparity leads to resentment and extreme disparity leads to desperation.*

innovative, and contribute more to society than others do. It is natural that greater production should produce greater wealth, but when the disparity becomes oppression and exploitation, resentment is inevitable. If a government causes everyone to have the same income, it must somehow take from those who are most productive and give to those who are least productive. That discourages high productivity and encourages low productivity. That was a major flaw of Communism. Complete equality is not desirable in any large organization or society. All this means there must be some disparity but not too much. The goal has to be staying in that acceptable range.

Karl Marx used "production" as an umbrella term including anything that made money, ranging from entire industries like manufacturing, agriculture, or transportation down to roadside stands where individuals sold their surplus garden vegetables. He taught that whoever owned production controlled society and inevitably made laws benefitting themselves and exploiting *The Many*.

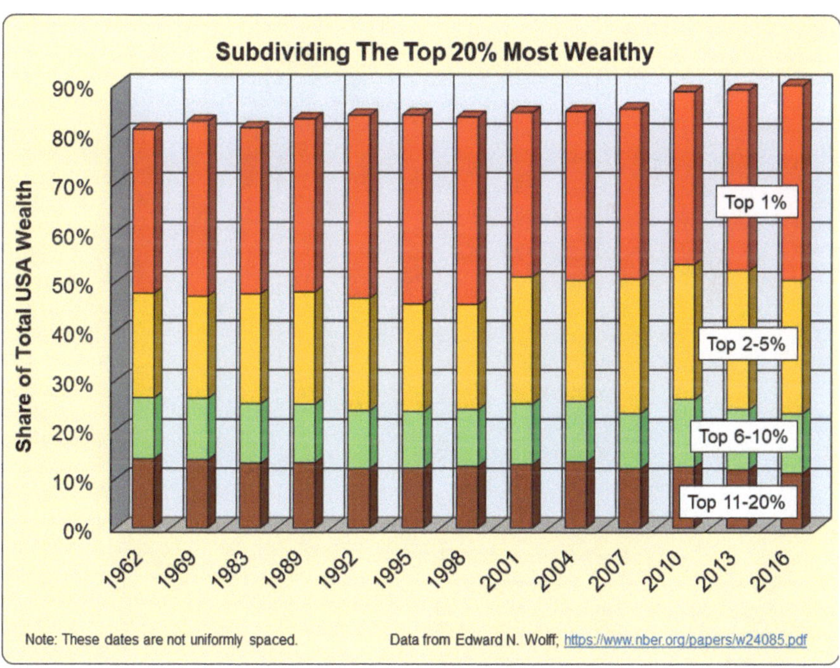

FIGURE 3 *Are those in the top 1% (99 percentile, Red above) are more comfortable or secure than those in the 80-90 percentile (Brown, above)? Note that the red bars represent well over a million households.*

Marx argued that the only way common people would ever have beneficial laws and economic systems would be to put those common people in power, and the only way for them to be in power was for them to own all production. *The Many* would need to seize and retain production by force because those who owned production would never voluntarily hand it over. Communist revolutions sprang up around the world, beginning in Russia in 1917, and they were violent.

When the Constitution was drafted, American industry was very different from what it is today. Agriculture was small farmers, and manufacturing was primarily individual craftsmen. Even the largest plantations of the South were tiny compared to today's corporations that control production and prices of agricultural products. The Iron Law of Oligarchies applies to industries, too, and their ultimate fate is the same as any other oligarchy. Family farms are already almost extinct and small business, even retail stores, are rapidly disap-

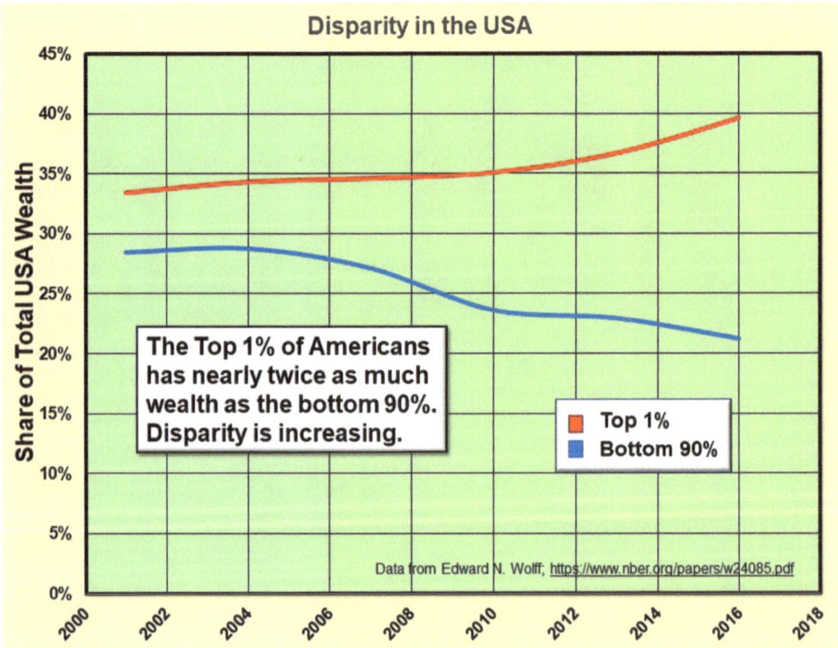

FIGURE 4 *The tax changes in 2017 apparently increased disparity but it won't be known by how much for some time. When combined with pandemic-related things like unemployment or evictions, medical disparity, bankruptcies, and racism, the situation is looking very dangerous.*

pearing. How long will it be before resentment becomes desperation and a triggering event sets off a revolution?

Communists quickly learned that seizing all production from its owners and keeping it requires military muscle and a strong leader with major discretionary power. Compelling citizens to turn over everything they produce to the government also requires force. A dictatorship is inevitable, and in order to suppress predictable rebellion, the dictator must be merciless. If *The Many* acquired all agriculture or manufacturing, for example, it would not be possible to manage an industry by pure democracy, and some sort of smaller group would be essential. Right back to the laws of oligarchy[14, 15], with oligarchs enriching themselves at the expense of *The Many* while maintaining their position through obsequious devotion to the strongman dictator and dealing out severe punishment for dissent. If that sounds a lot like the French Revolution, there were indeed many similarities. Think about the Russian and Chinese experience with Communism, as it was originally.

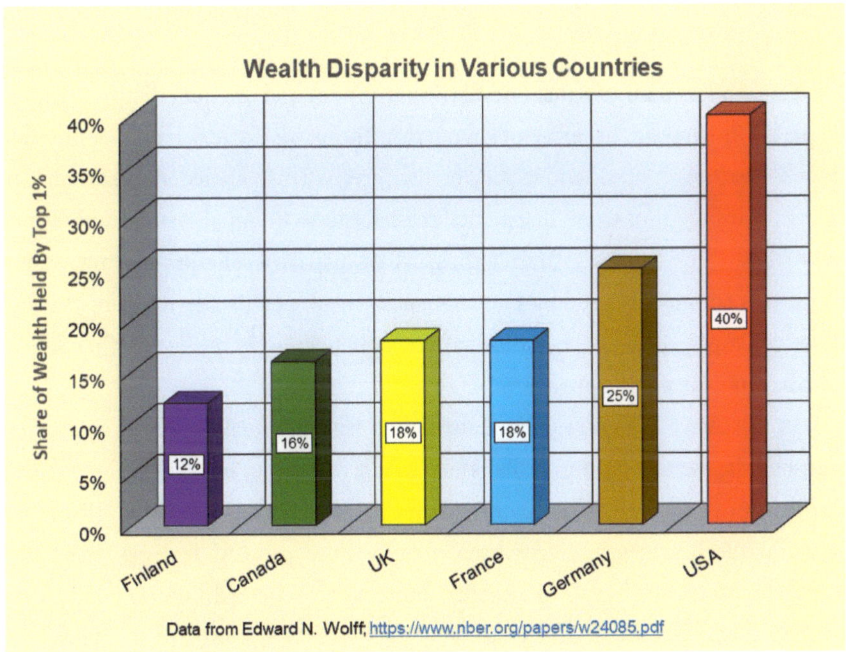

FIGURE 5 *The USA disparity grew during the Industrial Revolution when oligarchs had strong influence in getting legislation passed that favored large corporations and ultra-wealthy individuals. Those who favor deregulation and Supply Side Economics always have support of those who own production.*

It is easy to understand why Communism had such strong appeal in 1917 Russia. Peasants were not allowed to own the land they farmed, and all production was controlled by oligarchies, mostly The Church and The Aristocracy. Russia was a blend of Theocracy and Autocracy in 1917. Tours of Russian cathedrals and museums show the ruling class lived in opulent splendor while *The Many* were poverty stricken and on the brink of starvation. Communism began with the idealized objective of everyone having an equal and high standard of living but it didn't work as intended. The Commissars (by whatever name) in charge of production units or dispensing agencies immediately became powerful oligarchies that amplified problems stemming from compulsory "equalizing" efforts.

The Gini Coefficient

Oppression has many forms, but all of them reduce to unequal distribution or disparity. It may be disparity of ownership (housing, for example), resources (loans, insurance, etc.), education, healthcare, voting, justice systems, or job opportunities. All of these disparities contribute to unequal standard of living or wealth. There is a quantitative measure of disparity called the Gini Coefficient. It is commonly used by Economists to show wealth distribution, but the same concept can be used to illustrate or approximately measure other more abstract indicators of oppression.

In the chart in Figure 6, the purple line is total equality, where every citizen has the same holding. This is not really desirable, but it is a theoretical limit, where any 10% of the people would be the same as any other 10%.

The red line is actual distribution and yellow area "A" is disparity or cumulative difference between equality and reality. The red line boundary between yellow and blue in this chart only illustrates the point and is not a set of real data. An ideal wealth distribution would look much like this, however, with little or no poverty, a strong middle class, and enough disparity to provide incentive for outstanding production. Similar charts are drawn for resources, net worth, and income.

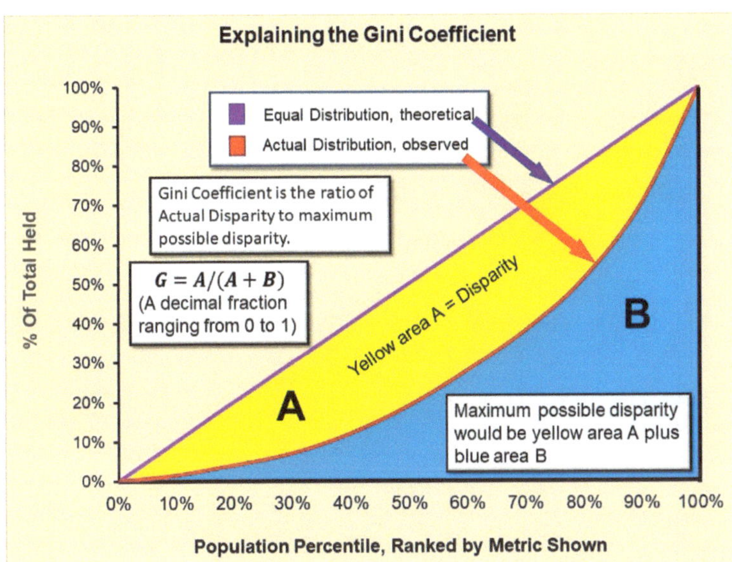

FIGURE 6 *The yellow area is disparity, and the Gini Coefficient is the decimal fraction of how large the disparity is compared to the maximum it could possibly be. This same mathematical process can be applied to disparities other than wealth, but all disparities, when extreme, cause resentment.*

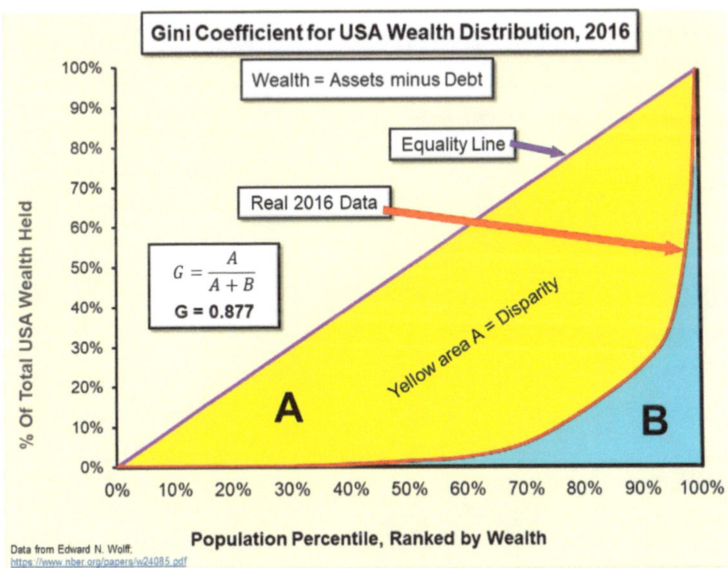

FIGURE 7 *It seems intuitively obvious that the cushion preventing chaos, blue area B, is dangerously small. Note that the 2017 changes in tax laws increased disparity by an unknown amount.*

Maximum possible disparity would occur if one person had all the measured quantity and everyone else had nothing. In practice this will not occur because *The Many* will revolt and force a regime change when the oppression gets so severe that they become desperate enough to risk their life to make things better. When tyrants take over a country and amass great personal power and wealth, they must surround themselves with loyal sycophants for their personal safety. Corruption that serious leads to a short time in power for the tyrant, often ending in violence against his supporters and great cost to *The Many* he or she rules.

Real American Data

So just how severe is economic disparity in our present-day America? Figure 7 is a Gini chart computation from 2016 data as analyzed by Dr. Edward Wolff,[19] a world-renowned economics expert at New York University. It is worth careful consideration, but it still does not give us a time when a revolution will begin, it only says we are moving in that direction and we don't have far to go.

Note that this 2016 data is before the tax changes of 2017 that increased disparity and the 2020 pandemic perturbations whose impact may not be clear for years to come. Also note this is not the only cause of revolutions, and oppression is a multi-component monster that cannot be attributed to a single measure. Several factors will combine to produce the desperation that pushes *The Many* into revolution.

There is a small inaccuracy in Figure 7, the 2016 Wealth Distribution chart. Actual distribution was slightly negative for the lowest 20-25% of the population but is shown here as zero to keep the graphical software from going crazy.

Root causes of the large and growing disparities in the USA include basic human greed, racism, and a system conducive to an oligarchy seizing control, thus ceding power to the most avaricious among us. Racism is a very serious source of economic disparity, but that is a complex subject that seems beyond the scope of this discussion. Readers should review the work of Dr. Wolff and others for scholarly examination of this subject.[20] For now just note that the

 CARL D. VELEY

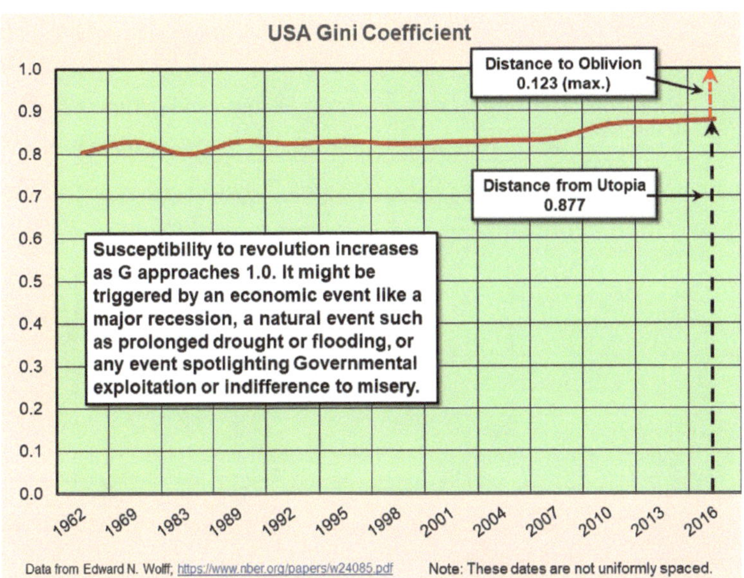

FIGURE 8 *As the Gini Coefficient continues to grow, the likelihood of a triggering event increases. If we continue to combine police brutality incidents with pandemic-related unemployment such an event becomes inevitable.*

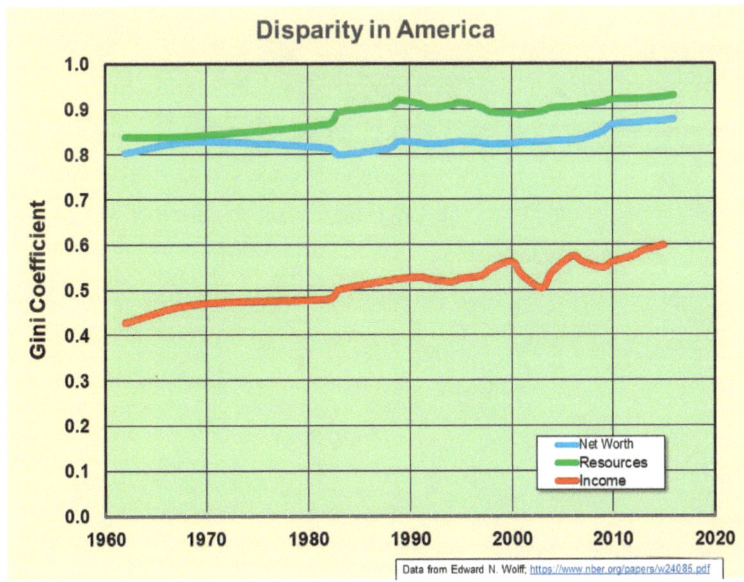

FIGURE 9 *There are many disparities contributing to insidious oppression in the USA. Among these are interest rates, housing, education, job opportunities, voting and other forms of discrimination, often but not always, based on racism.*

civil rights movements of the 1960s did not make racism disappear in the USA, but it did make it become less obvious and therefore more treacherous. It is a significant component of the lake of resentment that can become a flash flood of revolution if some grossly unfair event cracks the dam of acceptance. Think of the impact of events like Rosa Parks, George Floyd, or the many others that have drawn attention to laws and unequal enforcement practices.

Additional Exploitation

There is more to exploitation than economics. The rising outrage over police brutality against African-Americans stands as a powerful warning that resentment is just below the boiling point and just below the surface of society. It can realistically be argued that racism is a root cause of oppression leading relentlessly to revolution. Other forms of oppression include voting suppression, education inequalities, unequal justice, access to loans, healthcare, and employment, but they are dominated by, or heavily influenced by, racism, a belief that some races are intrinsically inferior.

Disparities that contribute to resentment and frustration of *The Many* include those in Figure 9 that can be represented by a variation of the Gini Coefficient. Other major disparities include healthcare, criminal justice, education, employment opportunities, and voting. Disparities are commonly linked to racism and can be difficult to measure quantitatively, but nonetheless contribute to resentment that eventually becomes revolution.

Recap

Part one reviewed how the Constitution's authors tried to construct a government where laws would be generated by ordinary people who carefully considered pro and con arguments. The Founding Fathers tried to avoid oligarchies by limiting terms of elected officials, and they intended for all laws

    CARL D. VELEY

to be in the best interests of the People, not just serving best interests of a ruling oligarchy. Their intentions have been foiled by technical developments, particularly in communication, that have made campaigning incredibly expensive and have morphed the Republic into a Plutocracy. It is time to review the Constitution to achieve its objectives in modern times.

Part two showed The USA is headed for a revolution that could occur at any time. When such a catastrophic event occurs, there is a high probability that those seizing power will be bent on retribution and not be prepared to prevent another oligarchy from taking over. This is additional incentive for updating the Constitution. It is an opportunity to correct the basic problem without the anguish of a revolution. It would be better to establish a real Democratic Republic peacefully than endure the horrors of violent revolution and chaos.

Part one shows Constitutional revisions would be beneficial to ordinary people and are essential for long-term stability. Revisions definitely will not be supported by the oligarchies, large corporations, and wealthy individuals benefitting from the present arrangements.

Part two shows how oligarchs who resist changes are putting themselves in danger because the present systems inevitably produce revolution. The probability is that a devastating revolution, possibly violent, will install a replacement government that will simply continue the oligarchy cycle without a permanent solution. Nobody can predict exactly when a revolution will begin or what will be required to trigger it, but the continuing series of incidents of unarmed African-Americans being killed by white police deserve attention. Racial disparity can combine with economic disparity to create a ubiquitous rage, largely out of sight, that provides the fuel for revolution and puts the oppressing oligarchies in grave physical danger.

Part three is intended as a starting point for discussing what can be done to avert the catastrophe of revolution and produce a government that actually represents the entire citizenry spectrum and makes laws based on the best thinking of ordinary people. Local, State, and Federal politicians are calling for "change," but they don't precisely specify what they want to change to. This is the change that will be necessary to avoid takeover by an oligarchy and assure all demographic groups have a proportional voice in passing laws after meaningful debate.

Part Three:

Correcting the Problems

Overview

The objective is a government that acts in the best interests of the entire population, based on clear reasoning of ordinary people. We propose building a new form of government based on these general assumptions:

Basic Assumptions

- ➤ All people want to make the world a better place, but they have sharply different opinions about what "better" means and the best ways to achieve that goal.

- ➤ All people, regardless of education, social status, or economic means, are susceptible to indoctrination via political message inculcations. They tend to consider political parties other than their own as treacherous <u>enemy</u> to be destroyed rather than loyal <u>opponent</u> to be debated, and ignore or actively oppose anything suggested by other parties, without thoughtful consideration. Political parties rely on demonization to advance their agendas and the country would be better off without political parties, as they currently exist.

- ➤ Congress, or any group of citizens, cannot "represent" unless it is "representative" of those for whom it acts. It must be demographically similar to the whole population to represent the whole population. For example if 10% of the population is very wealthy and they are roughly evenly divided between male and female, then we cannot claim a group is "representative" of the population if 40% are very wealthy, and all of them are men. Likewise it cannot possibly be "representative" if 20% of the population has income of less than $15,000 per year and not a single member of the "representative" group is from that income bracket. At the risk of seeming pedantic, white people may *advocate* for African-Americans, but they cannot actually *represent* them if they are not one of them. Ideal governments must have true representatives and not just advocates.

➤ There will always be some people with a get-a-bigger-hammer approach to all problems and others who are zero-coercion idealists. Both extremes are bona-fide political viewpoints and deserve to be addressed in debates, but neither these nor any other political philosophy, major or minor, should prevail without challenge.

➤ Voting should be by true representatives, who are as free as possible from the mental shackles of political indoctrinations and whose prejudices are mitigated by truth and multiple viewpoints.

➤ Candidates for technical positions must have the requisite technical qualifications, and candidates for legislative positions should have minimum qualification requirements at least as stringent as, but not the same as, those for public school teachers. Input during the formative years of children is very important, and fate of the country is at least as important.

Here is the skeleton of the proposed method of building on the above assumptions to generate a true democratic-republic where true representatives generate laws and policies that benefit the maximum number of citizens and minimize growth of oligarchies. Again this is offered only as a starting point for discussion and is not at all exhaustive.

1. Use a computer algorithm to draw voting district boundaries as nearly square as possible with equal population being the only criterion and no other demographic consideration. Redraw boundaries only after census or major populations shifts.

2. Produce and maintain a detailed database of all citizens, with provisions for any citizen to option out of the details and withdraw from any chance of being selected as a voter or office holder.

3. Use a computer algorithm to randomly select a panel of proxy voters, large enough to be demographically representative and small enough to be sequestered for a campaign/election. Those selected must have passed the basic exam required of all naturalized citizens and pass a basic, impartial, blind Voir Dire. Participation should be compulsory with exemptions granted only for good reason, like exemption from jury duty or military draft. Members of the voting panel should be well paid and harshly censured for any corruption or dereliction of duty.

4. Selected voters should not be publicly identified before the election process begins, and any attempt to intimidate, bribe, or pressure a voter should be treated the same as felony jury tampering and severely punished.

5. Use a second computer algorithm to randomly select two qualified candidates for each elective office. Confirm they are willing to serve if elected, and randomly select replacements for those who decline the position.

6. Convene a campaign/election meeting of the voter panel at a suitable venue, with housing. Limit outside access to voters, much like jury sequestering procedures.

7. Allow each candidate ample time to present their campaign message with appropriate testimony, data, or arguments, plus answer questions from a moderator appointed by the election board in charge.

8. Immediately after both nominees for an office have rested their case, voters should electronically cast their vote, with further deliberation only in the event of ties or less than some pre-determined, but very small percentage difference.

9.   Elected officials selected via this process have no campaign expenses, thus eliminating the most common source of corruption, and they have no obligations to a political party, freeing them for rational debate. Anyone attempting to intimidate, bribe, threaten, or in any way pressure a representative should be guilty of a serious felony and harshly punished.

10. Likewise any representative selected via this process should be swiftly and severely punished for soliciting or accepting any sort of reward for voting or any other action for the sole purpose of benefiting a vested interest.

11. Voter panels can decide local, state, and federal elections, but each panel only functions one calendar year. The campaign/election may last two weeks, for example, but when its elections are complete, the panel is dismissed and no member can serve on another panel for at least two years. Panels might be re-convened in the event of run-offs or special elections.

12. At the discretion of the election board conducting the election, candidates' identity and appearance may be kept from voters until after voting to reduce any potential influence of racism or prejudice. At no time during the "campaign" period should a candidate's race, religion, sexual orientation, or political party affiliations be disclosed. Their occupations, overall social and political philosophy, formal and informal education, and life experiences can be discussed in presentations or Q&A sessions.

13. Keep the checks and balances factors in the present Constitution but strengthen the enforcement aspects. It is imperative that it should not be possible for the Executive Branch to defy Congressional oversight, for example.

14. Strictly limit duties and powers of the Executive Branch to implementing laws and prohibit either the Judicial or Executive Branches from introducing or even proposing legislation, altering budgeted allocations, or initiating non-emergency military actions.

15. At the end of each election session, voters' performances should be evaluated by peer review, and those reviews should factor in to randomized selection for future voting panels, and as a qualification for elected office.

16. House and Senate members should likewise face anonymous reviews each year of their term by the Voter panels for that year. Favorable reviews would be necessary to qualify for reelection or for higher office.

Majority Opinions

What's the best way to find out what millions of people think? Let's consider a sports analogy and then apply inductive reasoning to go from specific to general principles.

Every October the World Series of baseball is held to determine which is the better team, the American League champion or the National League champion. Suppose before the games begin, we want to find out who Americans think is the better team. Would you want to gamble based on voting in the home city of either team? Not likely. Sentiments for the home team would skew the opinions and not be a reliable indicator of what all America thinks. Balloting all baseball fans in America would not be worth the enormous expense, so to answer the question, we would turn to polling.

There is rigorous mathematical proof that if we ask 600 fans across the country, at random, it is 95% certain that the cumulative reply would be within ±4% of the response we would get if we asked all of the millions of fans. There are two extremely important provisions though. One, all respondents must be knowledgeable baseball fans, and two, they must be selected <u>at random</u> from the entire population of baseball fans.[21] For example, we cannot rely on a poll if all respondents are from American League cities, or if a high percentage of respondents don't follow baseball and don't have knowledge of the teams' performance.

The same phenomena apply to polling controversial questions, like, "How do Americans feel about abortions?" or "Who would Americans prefer to be the next President?" or, "What are the best tax rates?" As with the hypothetical World Series question, balloting all eligible voters is extremely expensive, and as explained in part one of this document, these are hot topics in which most Americans have been heavily inculcated. Finding 600 who are not already close-minded on a controversial subject would be hard, if not impossible. Even if we polled 1,000,000 registered voters at random, we still would not have a reliable measure of what clear-headed and well-informed Americans think because simply polling at random would not be a reliable indication of what those same respondents would decide if they had somehow been compelled to consider opposing viewpoints.

Polling more accurately reflected will of the voters than balloting did in the 2016 national elections. Despite campaign tactics involving malicious inuendo, outright falsehoods, and meddling by foreign countries, Hillary Clinton was still leading in the polls and indeed got about 3,000,000 more votes nationwide than Trump, but she nonetheless lost the election. This was because of antiquated and unfair methods of allocating Electoral College votes. Similar chicanery manipulates who votes, how voting districts are drawn (Gerrymandering) and truthfulness of campaign messages.

Voting and polling are both incapable of determining the best rational decisions if all voters have been inculcated by heavily biased partisan sources. Liberals get their news from liberal sources while Conservatives stick to conservative sources. The worst possible way to learn what the other party thinks is to listen exclusively to your own party propaganda. A Conservative will never get an accurate analysis of what Liberals think by asking another Conservative, and Liberals cannot learn what Conservatives teach by listening exclusively to Liberal commentators.

The main point is, polling, properly conducted, produces the same result as voting, provided the voting is also properly conducted. Neither is a reliable indicator of what indoctrinated citizens would conclude if they were not indoctrinated and were fully informed. We now turn to steps we can take to minimize impact of indoctrination and cause poll respondents to consider all pertinent information and viewpoints. If we can do that, we can replace voting with a cheaper, faster, and more democratic system than we have now – a greatly improved and more reliable form of polling than is generally possible today.

Proxy Voting

Ideally voters would be insulated from the fervor of zealous fanatics and calmly consider all aspects of an issue before casting a ballot. That is impossible with millions of voters, including zealots unwilling or unable to consider other viewpoints, and a barrage of inculcating campaigns advancing dubious information and arguments. It is possible with a small number of proxy voters who can be isolated and compelled to at least listen to pertinent arguments on all sides of issues. That does NOT mean a proxy system like those used by corporation shareholder meetings, it means a system more like that of selecting jurors. Its value would depend on defining the pool from which voters are drawn, filtering out those who are unsuited, insulating them from zealotry, presenting them with all applicable viewpoints, and obtaining the *reasoned* opinion of a non-inculcated, representative, random sampling of *The Many*.

Nothing is more important to any society than its justice system. The need for a system of laws to replace whims of despotic rulers was recognized nearly 4,000 years ago when the Code of Hammurabi was issued in ancient Mesopotamia. It was harsh – "Eye for eye, and tooth for tooth" – but it established rules defining crimes and punishments that did not vary with the severity of the king's hangover. Establishing the rule of law is a big step toward empowering *The Many* and limit-

> **KING JOHN**
>
> Have you noticed there is only one King John of England and no John II or John III? That's probably because no King wants to be named after the one who is widely believed to be the worst of all UK kings. He signed the Magna Carta under duress, then refused to abide by it. He was the "Bad King" in the Robin Hood stories and he managed to lose the royal jewels in October, 1216, among his many personal failings.

ing discretionary power of *The Few*. It will therefore be opposed by oligarchies, whose natural priority will always be increasing their power by making rules that benefit themselves.

A major advance in the rule of law came in 1215 when King John of England was forced to sign the Magna Carta, agreeing that everyone, including the king, must obey laws, and all citizens had rights that must be honored. It was the beginning of two very important pillars of modern governments – parliaments where ordinary people make the laws, and juries where the fate of ordinary people charged with a crime is decided by a group of their peers, not an all-powerful ruler.

The objective of a jury system is getting the judgement that a majority of ordinary people would produce if they considered all the pertinent facts and arguments. It is clearly not possible to get the opinion of all ordinary people, so it is necessary to select a small number of representatives and then minimize their prejudices and inculcations to get their reasoned conclusions. In broad terms, that requires randomly drawing prospective jurors from a pool of ordinary people, then filtering out those who are, or might be, biased for or against either plaintiff or defendant, those who are incapable of analytical reasoning for some reason, or those with a vested interest in the outcome.

When these representatives of "ordinary people" are assembled, they are compelled to hear and consider all significant facts and arguments before making their decision. It is rare for the public to dispute a jury's verdict, but when such disputes do arise, it generally is because the public did not hear all the evidence and made their decision based on incomplete or inaccurate news media reports.

Voting versus Polling

Internet news sites often conduct polls to find out how their followers feel about some controversial issue. Not surprisingly conservative sites find their followers have strongly conservative opinions, while liberal sites find their followers have strong liberal views, but neither one accurately determines what

  CARL D. VELEY

the total population thinks. Neither poll can determine what their respondents would think if they actually listened to and considered opposing opinions. People tend to listen to viewpoints that reinforce what they already believe and ignore those that disagree, creating a self-induced inculcation. That casts doubt on polling by any organization with biased members. Zealots and strongly inculcated people may also be more inclined to participate in voluntary polls, thus making the results less likely to reflect the views of the same respondents if they participated in honest, thoughtful, debate presenting multiple viewpoints.

If conducted properly, polls can accurately determine what a large group thinks without asking all members of the group.[21] The critical requirement is making a truly random sampling of the entire group. For large populations, polling a relatively small number will produce accurate results. For example, suppose we want to know how 100 million American voters would answer if we asked the question, "Should we _____?" If we select 600 voters <u>at random</u> and ask them, we can be 95% certain that their cumulative vote will be within ±4% of the vote we would get if we asked all 100 million voters the same question. For example, if 384 (64%) of the 600 respondents said "Yes" to the question, we can be 95% certain that if we asked all 100 million, between 60,000,000 (that's 64% minus 4%, or 60%) and 68,000,000 (that's 64% plus 4% or 68%) would answer "Yes." The same conclusions would apply if the total population is any large number. In fact as the subject population shrinks to 150,000 or fewer, the sample size needed slowly gets smaller than 600. This can be mathematically proved and is not guesswork, but the critical steps are making sure the respondents are from the subject population and were selected randomly (It is recommended that readers who are not familiar with statistical analysis go to interactive site: https://www.surveysystem.com/sscalc.htm#one and experiment a little to get acquainted with the concepts).

Most of our current State and Federal representatives are so indebted to their party and financial supporters that they reflexively reject any and all proposals from the opposition party, resist compromise, and avoid actual debate. It is hard to prove scientifically, but it seems reasonable to assume that our representatives do NOT reason like ordinary Americans would reason if they were not inculcated and could somehow be compelled to consider all the pros and cons of issues. We would be better off selecting representatives who we could be 95% sure think the way ordinary people would think if they could be freed from their inculcations and prejudices.

Suppose those representatives also duplicated demographics of the whole population, meaning if 30% of the adult population is Catholic and 1.5% are Jewish, then roughly 30% and 1.5% of the representatives should also be Catholic and Jewish respectively. If 50% of the population are women, then 50% of the representatives should also be women, and all income ranges should be represented in the same proportion as in the population and so forth. That would be a Democratic-Republic the Constitution's framers intended but could not create with 1787 technology or envision with 1787 social standards. It is possible in the 21st century.

Step One, Create Databases and Qualifying Tests

First, broaden the USA Social Security database to include additional information, such as education, profession, work experience, and scores on at least two tests – a *Civics Test* and a *Basic Logic Test*. It should not be necessary to pass a test to get a passport or receive Social Security benefits, but it should be a minimum requirement for voting or holding public office. American citizens wanting to abstain from political processes can simply refuse to take the tests, and test scores would only be entered via the official automated test process. Additional fields in this database would include public positions held or services performed, such as jury duty, School Board, City Council, law enforcement, or military service.

Test Scores

Voting can be considered a right, a privilege, or a duty. The United States is one of just eleven constitutional Democracies that consider voting a privilege and not a right guaranteed in their Constitution.[22, 23, 24] Australia considers voting a duty and makes it compulsory, with fines for not voting. Voting booths are even set up in prisons. Currently to register to vote in the USA Federal elections one must:

- ➤ Be a USA citizen by birth or naturalization

- ➤ Meet their State's residency requirements

- ➤ Be eighteen-years-old or older

- ➤ Not be in prison or on parole for a felony

Ironically, the naturalization process requires basic civics knowledge and qualities of good citizenship while citizens by birth have no such requirement for voting. It would be possible for someone born in the USA to register to vote, despite not speaking English, having no knowledge of US history or government functions, and having primary loyalty to a country other than The United States. Requiring birthright citizens to meet the same standards as naturalized citizens for voting rights would reduce the number of poorly informed, inculcated, and zealous voters. That alone would be an improvement.

Juries Should Not Deliberate

In criminal trials, the question before the jury is not, "Is the accused guilty?" It is, "Did the prosecutors prove guilt?" If at the end of the courtroom proceedings a juror has a reasonable doubt, then the answer for that juror is "No", but if the jury then deliberates and other jurors argue forcefully and cause the hesitant juror to change his or her mind, then the verdict is based on what happened in the jury room, not in the open courtroom where knowledgeable experts challenge assertions and arguments. For an uncontaminated verdict, the jurors would cast a secret ballot at the end of courtroom proceedings, with no deliberation, answering the question, "Did the prosecution prove their accusations beyond reasonable doubt?" This would remove extraneous influence on the process, but to assure validity the jurors would need to pass a basic test demonstrating they think logically.

We require everyone to pass a computerized exam to get a driver's license. For an ordinary license, the exam is about basic rules of the road, but more advanced exams are required for people driving heavy trucks or buses or hauling hazardous materials. We do not hear serious complaints that the tests are biased, and the consensus opinion is that they are necessary to assure drivers have the essential minimum knowledge. Why not have a similar requirement for voting and other political activities?

If a man is tried for a crime, a pool of prospective jurors is assembled and undergoes a process known as *voir dire* to establish their suitability for deciding his fate. Shouldn't we have a similar process to establish suitability for deciding the fate of the country? We already have such a requirement for naturalized citizens, why not require native born citizens to be equally well informed before granting them the privilege of participating in government?[25] It would be a simple matter to devise a computerized *voir dire* to qualify prospective voters with basic Civics and Logic quizzes. Family or business entanglements should also be noted as potential conflicts of interest.

Citizens must never be required to pass a test to enjoy their *rights* as guaranteed by the Constitution, but it is fair to demand they qualify for *privileges*. Nobody has a *right* to drive a car, potentially causing serious harm to others. Driving is a *privilege* granted only to people who can first demonstrate knowledge of the rules and then comply with those rules. We also require tests and compliance for people who want a license (privilege) to work at a host of professions, including medicine, law, public accounting, or trades, such electrician, plumber, pilot, barber, code welder, and many

> ## Voir Dire
>
> (vwahr [with a near-silent "r"] deer) n. from French "to see to speak." The questioning of prospective jurors by a judge and attorneys in court.
>
> Voir dire is used to determine if a juror is biased and/or cannot deal with the issues fairly, or if there is cause not to allow a juror to serve (knowledge of the facts; friendship with parties, witnesses or attorneys; an occupation or avocation that might lead to bias; prejudice for or against possible jury actions; or past experiences such as having been sued in a similar case).
>
> https://dictionary.law.com/Default.aspx?selected=2229

others. Strictly speaking people have a *right* to a *privilege* as long as they comply with requirements and the requirements are unbiased and reasonable. A vote has intrinsic potential for causing public harm if cast in ignorance or malice, and the public has a right to require voters to meet minimum standards of knowledge and logic but no right to dictate an opinion or set irrelevant requirements, such as race, ethnicity, religion, fee payments, gender or sexual orientation, hair style, political viewpoint, or clothing preferences.

Testing centers could be established in conjunction with Driver's License offices, polling places, libraries, schools, or wherever is convenient. Citizens should have the right to take, or refuse to take, any of the standard tests, including basics of: 1) Civics, 2) Logic, 3) History, 4) Economics, 5) Legal, and 6) Ethics. Tests should not require advanced or specialized education on the subject matter.

Tests would be generated by committees of university professors expert in such testing. Each committee member would serve one four-year term with staggered terms such that half the members are replaced each two years. Professors assigned to the Committee would continue to be paid by their respective universities with the government compensating the university for the professor's time away from his or her regular duties. The committee would generate lists of questions from which a computer would randomly select questions to compose a quiz for each applicant. For example, if they generate a list of 200 questions, and when an applicant takes a test, a computer selects twenty questions at random from that list, the odds are roughly $2.11\mathrm{x}10^{46}$ to 1 against any two tests being exactly alike. That should cut down on cheating when taking the exam, and if the applicant manages to get the list and study until he knows correct answers for all 200 questions, that's exactly what we want in voters.

Applicants' scores would be recorded in the database along with other demographic data, such as education, technical specialties, and work experience. The test scores would be one criterion in generating tables from which proxy voters and candidates for office would be randomly selected by carefully controlled computers. Standard database techniques would produce pools from which prospects would be selected. For example, members selected for the committees devising tests would have to be shown in the database as being university professors with expertise in devising and interpreting tests. To be included in the pool from which voters are drawn, people would only need to meet age and citizenship requirements, plus passing scores on basics of civics and logic.

Step Two – Revise Duties of Election Boards

Election Boards should be tasked with finding out what citizens think about subject matters when they are fully informed, are free of inaccurate inculcations, and rationally consider pros and cons of issues. Stop holding elections with millions of inculcated people voting. Instead hold proxy votes. Use simple computer algorithms to randomly select at least 600 qualified voters (who passed at least the Civics and Logic tests described previously) in each state, sequester them in a resort, and prepare them for voting by reducing the effects of inculcation and party bias. Participation should be compulsory, like the military draft of the World War II era, or contemporary jury duty summons. Restrict outside communications as for a sequestered trial jury, require them to attend presentations, pro and con, on all issues or candidates on the ballot, then, without further deliberation, register their votes. The subject matter could be anything that is currently put on a ballot.

Stepwise, Election Boards would need to:

> Maintain databases of qualified voters in computer drawn districts, as nearly as possible square in shape and enclosing an equal number of resident qualified voters, without regard to demographic or political factors.

> The total number of political units (districts or precincts) would remain the same as now but objectively drawn by computer to eliminate gerrymandering.

> Using an objective computer algorithm, randomly select enough qualified voters to form a pool of voters, large enough to produce

results with confidence level of 95% and a confidence interval of ±4% or better.

➤ Organize and conduct proxy votes, instead of elections wherein all eligible voters cast a ballot. A proxy vote process would be patterned after the criminal jury trial procedures where all members of the pool have already cleared *voir dire* and must listen attentively to arguments pro and con (like the prosecution and defense arguments in a trial) before casting a ballot without further deliberation.

➤ Record the results of the proxy vote as results for the entire District, as if 100% of eligible voters had cast a ballot. For example, if there are 200,000 eligible voters in the District and the proxy vote is 60% "Yes" and 40% "No", record the results as 120,000 "Yes" and 80,000 "No" votes.

➤ For subsets of the district's voters, city or county questions, for example, it is ordinary database programing to randomly select 600 qualified voters who also meet the residency requirements.

➤ If the subset is small, perhaps a school district election or a bond issue, the number of proxy voters should be sufficient to attain a 95% confidence level with a margin of error of 4%. Alternatively it may be best to simply hold a conventional vote.

➤ Coordinate with other election boards as necessary to produce meaningful State or Federal votes.

Pay these proxy voters well and require employers to give time off, as in jury duty rules. Be reluctant to excuse those selected for proxy duty, but when it is absolutely necessary, select a replacement at random, by computer, who is demographically similar to the excused proxy. Election Board personnel should conduct proxy education sessions

Setting Voting Districts

Gerrymandering is a lethal enemy of Democracy. It is a powerful tactic used by ruling oligarchies to perpetuate their hold on power, and it thwarts the very foundation of democracy – majority rule. A review of literature on Gerrymandering shows its role in building resentment that will eventually lead to revolution. Here is an example of how Gerrymandering distorted voting in the 2018 mid-terms.[26] This is just one example, but it resulted in a swing of seven votes away from the will of the people.

	Vote Democrat	Vote Republican	No. Seats in Congress	Elected Representatives	
North Carolina	48.35%	50.39%	13	D Fair = 6 D Actual = 3	R Fair = 7 R Actual = 10
Ohio	47.27%	52%	16	D Fair = 8 D Actual = 4	R Fair = 8 R Actual = 12

Gerrymandering began with Elbridge Gerry in 1812 and has been used by all political parties since. A notable example was shortly after the Civil War. Republicans were in power and determined admission of new States. Instead of admitting Dakota territory as one State, they divided it into two states because Electoral College rules allocated a minimum of three votes to a State regardless of how sparsely populated it was. Dakota was Republican leaning and this division gave them six Electoral Votes instead of three. If votes had been prorated by population, one Dakota State might have had only one.[27] Slate Magazine offers a light-hearted game that illustrates the deadly serious harm of Gerrymandering.[28]

Voting districts should be drawn by computer as nearly as possible in rectangular shapes, and reasonably close to equal voting populations with no other demographic criteria. Overlapping districts, such as city, county, school district, and so forth, can easily be handled when selecting proxy voters by computer.

Enacting These Changes

We can be sure politicians in power will vehemently object to any changes in the process that brought them to power. Oblivious to exploitation and suppression, they will insist the present Constitution has worked well for over 200 years. Change this significant will probably only occur after a revolution, and maybe not even then. If it does, it should begin with assembling a Constitutional Convention, like the one in 1787.[29] Participants should include Constitutional scholars, historians, IT specialists, Civil Rights leaders, labor leaders, lawyers and judges, but sitting politicians should be excluded. Conventioneers should consider the philosophy and intent of these suggestions but not be bound by any specific point.

Conclusions

There are many advantages in replacing traditional voting with proxy votes by qualified voters randomly selected and presented with all relevant considerations.

1. Huge savings in cost

    a. Cost of the actual balloting, city, county, State, and Federal

    b. Eliminate campaign expenses borne by candidates

    c. Greatly reduce the incessant fund-raising by political entities

2. Cut campaign time from a year or two, directed to the whole population down to a day or two, directed at a small captive audience

3. Reduce incessant fund-raising of political parties, candidates, and action groups.

4. Combat inculcation that contaminates and misleads voters

5. Get input and opinions from the full spectrum of citizens

6. Greatly reduce corruption and the effects of money on selecting representatives

7. Avoid all forms of oligarchy

8. Assure voters are fully informed on the pros and cons of issues or candidates

9. Make it possible for ordinary people to hold office without obligations to special interests or indebtedness to political parties

10. Increase involvement of rational people who currently abstain from "dirty" politics

11. Prevent Gerrymandering and other anti-democratic voting manipulations

12. Select candidates and representatives based on qualifications instead of obsessions

13. Create the Democratic-Republic sought in 1787

Endnotes

1.   https://en.wikipedia.org/wiki/Category:Revolutions

2.   https://en.wikipedia.org/wiki/Canning#History_and_development_of_canning

3.   https://en.wiktionary.org/wiki/Category:English_words_suffixed_with_-cracy

4.   https://en.wikipedia.org/wiki/Kakistocracy

5.   https://www.historyisfun.org/yorktown-victory-center/militia-in-the-revolutionary-war/

6.   https://teachingamericanhistory.org/library/document/orders-from-general-thomas-gage-to-lieut-colonel-smith-10thregiment-foot/

7.   https://en.wikipedia.org/wiki/1788%E2%80%9389_United_States_presidential_election#Results_by_state

8.   https://en.wikipedia.org/wiki/Timeline_of_voting_rights_in_the_United_States

9.   https://www.greatbigcanvas.com/view/the-boston-massacre-engraving-by-paul-revere,2141342/?gclid=Cj0KCQiAtf_tBRDtARIsAIbAKe2lHxld565FCKnj5R3z6OQSzNMyK-Lvo_4TMzziiRRGDFj6dDy1N0j0aAgQ6EALw_wcB

10.   https://www.history.com/topics/mexican-american-war

11.   https://history.state.gov/milestones/1866-1898/yellow-journalism
https://www.britannica.com/topic/yellow-journalism

12.   https://en.wikipedia.org/wiki/The_Octopus:_A_Story_of_California

13.   https://www.opensecrets.org/overview/cost.php

14.   https://en.wikipedia.org/wiki/Iron_law_of_oligarchy

15.   https://en.wikipedia.org/wiki/Oligarchy

16.   https://en.wikipedia.org/wiki/Category:20th-century_revolutions

17.   https://en.wikipedia.org/wiki/List_of_revolutions_and_rebellions#1900s

18. https://en.wikipedia.org/wiki/Ludlow_Massacre

19. https://www.nber.org/papers/w24085

20. http://www.levyinstitute.org/publications/the-great-recession-and-racial-inequali-tyevidence-from-measures-of-economic-well-being

21. https://www.surveysystem.com/sscalc.htm#one

22. https://www.fairvote.org/right_to_vote_amendment

23. https://www.uscis.gov/citizenship/educators/naturalization-information

24. https://democracyjournal.org/magazine/28/the-missing-right-a-constitutional-right-tovote/

25. https://www.uscis.gov/citizenship/educators/naturalization-information#natz_test

26. https://en.wikipedia.org/wiki/Gerrymandering_in_the_United_States

27. https://en.wikipedia.org/wiki/Gerrymandering#cite_note-120

28. https://slate.com/news-and-politics/2020/06/gerrymander-puzzle-missouri.html

29. https://history.state.gov/milestones/1784-1800/convention-and-ratification

Appendix

Here are stepwise instructions for a simple simulator illustrating how random selections are made by computers. For a real selection, more elaborate programs would be needed to process millions of voters in a database. It would still follow this basic process, and these instructions assume readers have only basic Excel skills.

Start with a blank worksheet. Yours will have more rows and columns than this.

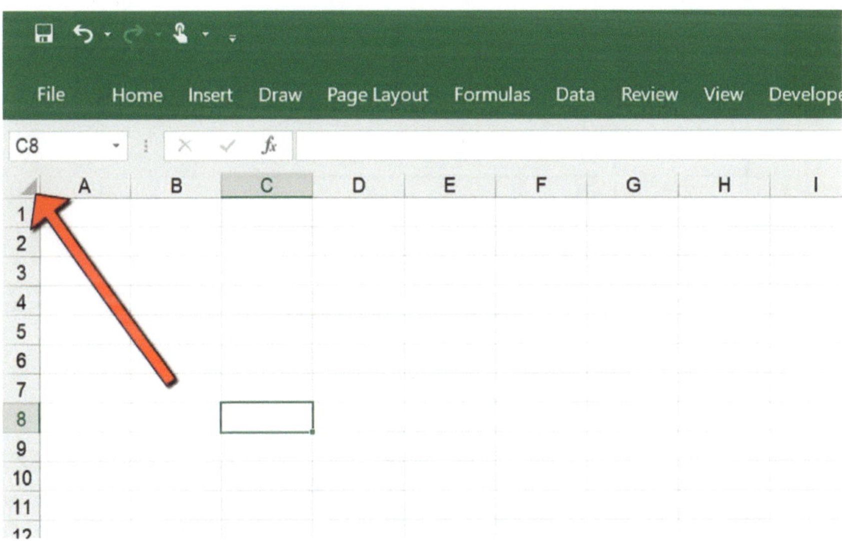

1. Click on the little triangle indicated by the red arrow, to select the whole worksheet.

    a. Right click on any cell in the selected (gray) area,

        i.   from the drop-down list that appears set Row Height to 15,
        ii. (optional: set font to Arial, 12 point.) click Format Cells>Alignment>set text alignment to Center both vertical and horizontal.

iii. Click anywhere to de-select the sheet.

b. Place the mouse cursor on the "A" above the first column, hold the left button down and drag to column E. This selects the first five columns.

   i. Right click on any cell.

   ii. From the drop-down list, set column width to 18.

2. Make the following entries. Cells on row 2 must be **exactly** as shown

In Cell:	Type this:
A1	No. Eligible Citizens
B1	SSN
C1	Random No.
D1	Rank
E1	Selected
A4	No. to Select
A7	No. to Select
A8	=COUNT($E$2:$E$10000)
A2	=COUNTA($B$2:$B$10000)
B2	100100001
C2	=IF((B2<>""),RAND(),"")
D2	=IF((C2<>""),RANK(C2,$C$2:$C$10000))
E2	=IF((D2<>""),IF((D2<=$A$5),$B2,""),"")

3. Formatting certain cells makes the simulator easier to understand. To format column B, click on the letter B at the top of the column. Then, to de-select cell B1, hold down the Ctrl key and click on cell B1. That selects all of column B except cell B1. Repeat this when formatting each of the columns to exclude their headings.

Column	Actions
B	Select all B cells except B1>Right click any selected cell>Format Cells>Number>Special>Social Security Number
C	Select all C cells except C1>right click any selected cell>Format Cells>Number>Number>Decimal Places = 15
D	[Same as C but set Decimal Places to zero]
E	[Same as B]

4. Conditional Formatting all Cells in column E (Selected as above)

   a. On the Home tab, Styles group, click Conditional Formatting

   b. On drop-down list, click Highlight Cell Rules, then More Rules

   c. Another drop-down list, under Rule Type, click Format only cells that contain

   d. Also click from the list, under Format Only Cells With, click No Blanks

   e. Click Format>Font>Clear Strikethrough>Color=White

   f. Click Format>Fill=Red

5. Your spreadsheet should now look like this:

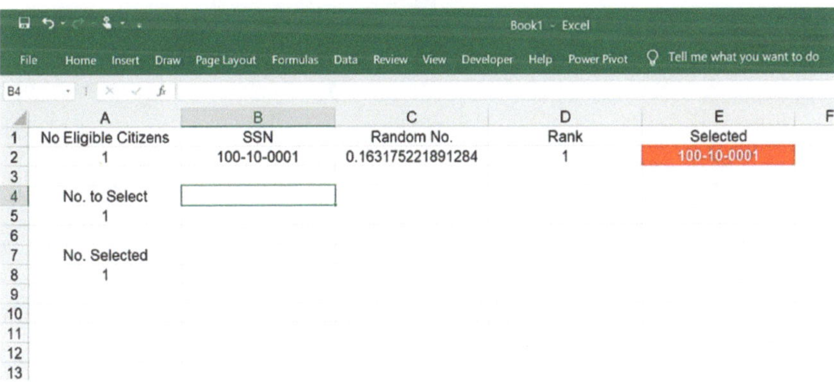

6. Enter artificial SSNs to see how this works.

   a. Put the cursor in cell B2, hold down the left mouse button and drag straight right to cell E2. This selects the four cells B2, C2, D2, and E2. There is a box drawn around the four cells and a small black dot in the lower right-hand corner of that box.

   b. Put the cursor on that dot and when it turns into a small black + sign, hold down the left mouse button and drag all four cells down to row 21.

   c. Now, your spreadsheet should look like this, but columns C, D, and E will have different numbers:

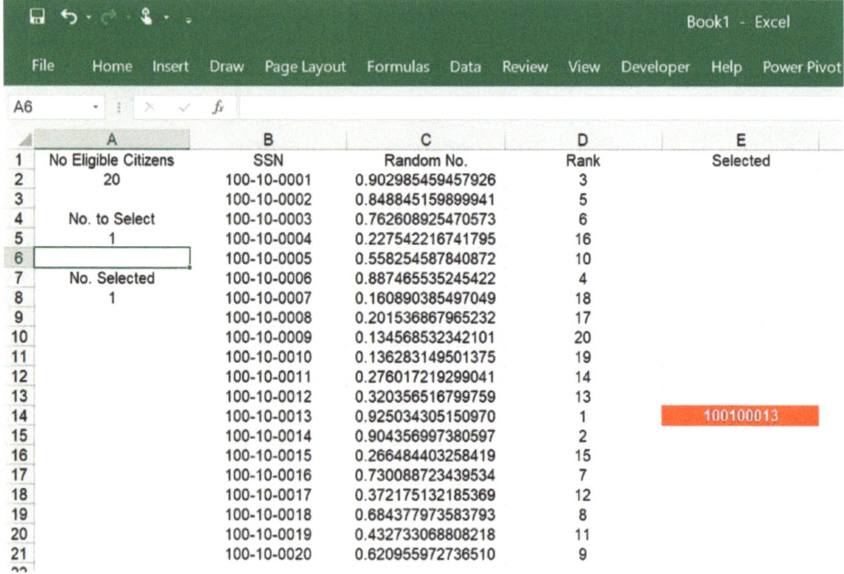

	A	B	C	D	E
1	No Eligible Citizens	SSN	Random No.	Rank	Selected
2	20	100-10-0001	0.902985459457926	3	
3		100-10-0002	0.848845159899941	5	
4	No. to Select	100-10-0003	0.762608925470573	6	
5	1	100-10-0004	0.227542216741795	16	
6		100-10-0005	0.558254587840872	10	
7	No. Selected	100-10-0006	0.887465535245422	4	
8	1	100-10-0007	0.160890385497049	18	
9		100-10-0008	0.201536867965232	17	
10		100-10-0009	0.134568532342101	20	
11		100-10-0010	0.136283149501375	19	
12		100-10-0011	0.276017219299041	14	
13		100-10-0012	0.320356516799759	13	
14		100-10-0013	0.925034305150970	1	100100013
15		100-10-0014	0.904356997380597	2	
16		100-10-0015	0.266484403258419	15	
17		100-10-0016	0.730088723439534	7	
18		100-10-0017	0.372175132185369	12	
19		100-10-0018	0.684377973583793	8	
20		100-10-0019	0.432733068808218	11	
21		100-10-0020	0.620955972736510	9	

7. Press the F9 key several times. The sheet recalculates each time. Change cell A5 to another number, less than the number in A2. Press the F9 key again to see the computer select as many as you asked for in cell A5.

8. Select cells B21, C21, D21, and E21. Drag them down to row 1001. You can drag them to any row you want, up to 10,000, but 1,000 is plenty to experiment by selecting different numbers of voters, and pressing the F9 key.

How it Works

A real program would be part of a sophisticated database with real voter ID numbers, not these artificial SSNs. Cells in column C generate a random number, a decimal fraction ranging between zero and one. It will never be zero and never be 1.0 and it calculates to 15 decimal places. The next column, D, determines rank of the random number beside it. That is, if we sorted the entire C column, smallest to largest, where would this one stand. Finally, each cell in the E column checks to see if its rank (the adjacent cell) is equal to or less than the number in cell A5. In other words, if the assignment is to pick A5 voters at random, this spreadsheet generates a random number for each voter, sorts them in order of smallest random number to largest, and marks the voter IDs having random numbers equal to or smaller than A5.